WHOLE

WHOLE

11 UNIVERSAL TRUTHS FOR
AN INSPIRED LIFE

PAMELA PUJA KIRPALANI

 Leadstart

ISBN: 978-93-90266-38-8
Copyright © Pamela Puja Kirpalani, 2020
Cover Design: Ashwini Jadhav
Layout: Hitanshi Shah
Printing: Nutech

Published in India 2021 by
Leadstart
A Division of One Point Six Technologies Pvt Ltd
119-123, Building J2, Shram Seva Premises
Wadala (East), Mumbai 400 022, Maharashtra, INDIA
T + 91 96 99933000   **E** info@leadstartcorp.com
W www.leadstartcorp.com

Vishal, for all the truth you have made me see, in every single way.

Samara, for encouraging me to begin this journey in the first place.

And Yaash, for our night time conversations and your deep insights,

I am forever grateful.

In Eternity,
Puja

ABOUT THE AUTHOR

PAMELA PUJA KIRPALANI, a globally seasoned Trainer & Coach runs the highly acclaimed Inner High Living in Singapore, an NLP Consulting & Coaching Practice. She spends her time training world-class companies and private groups in scientific Persuasion & Non-Verbal Communication workshops, coaching clients using Neuro Linguistic Programming techniques, and writing for various global publications. The crux of her writing lies in her ability to relate heart-to-heart with her audience while integrating the latest social and neuroscience research. She is a gritty optimist with perfectionist tendencies, and a mother of two inspiring children. Her work has been featured on Elephant Journal, BBC World, Deccan Herald, and The Economic Times amongst others.

Contents

HAPPINESS
OUR CULTURAL OBSESSION

"Like a lion placed in a paper cage, human beings are trapped by the illusions of their own mind"
Russ Harris, *The Happiness Trap*

It takes an art to capture into words - the irony, the beauty and the complexities of the human mind. Blessed with the human faculty to contemplate and rationalise, every day we are plagued by so many questions...Why am I here? What is my purpose? Why am I in this job? What are my talents? How can I be happy?

And the human mind is marvellous in response. The prefrontal cortex part of our brain, responsible for all rational and analytical decisions, plays a large role in helping us navigate our lives and putting things into reasonable perspective. It tells us how we can avoid pain; who we should stay away from; what motivates us day-to-day; what the next big opportunity is; and so much more.

Alas, despite all the logical benefits we receive from our advanced brain faculties - much unlike any other species existent on the human planet - we forget that our mind can also be our biggest adversary.

Why? Firstly, our brain is designed to convince us that all the thoughts in our mind form the basis of our 'reality', and because of this phenomenon we are left with no choice but to believe everything that our thoughts tell us. And there is good reason for this too. In fact, on a biological level, the effect of a single thought is so powerful that every time it is activated, a unique biochemical reaction courses through our bodies, guised in the form of a feeling or emotion. These thoughts repeated over and over again, eventually become a part of our everyday engrained belief systems. And without us even being consciously aware, these belief systems transform into our very own rose-tinted glasses that form the foundation of how we see others, how we see ourselves and how we think living a happy life should be. But in truth, even though we believe all our thoughts to be 'real' - everything we perceive around us is of course a result of the opinions and reactions of people close to us and also our own past experiences from our childhood.

And so naturally, these set of thoughts that define you and I have eventually become a set of stories guiding us on how we should be living our lives. Now, not all stories are bad - some serve us well and help us in day-to-day subsistence and general well-being. But after a while, we come to realise that we do not have a conscious control over them. As we grow older and become adults, our view of the world and of people around us becomes more and more fixed, as we gently succumb to these deeply engrained belief systems. As it happens, they run ever so subtly under our unconscious radar from the minute we wake up to the time we are asleep.

So, what do these undercurrent belief systems do for us?

They tell us who we are, what we should do, how we should be, and how we should be happy.

They convince us that our limitations are too strong and fool us into underestimating our potential.

They map an internal world that makes us believe that taking up a challenge is much too risky.

They create distance between people because of fear.

We know that these systems are real because as babies and toddlers, we are of pure thought and largely unconditioned by society's dogma. With no set belief systems or fixed notions of the world around us - we run purely on our other powerful faculty-our instinct. In fact, it is believed that as babies we also rely purely on our essential genetic core nature - which usually comprises of the effects of knowledge and experience from generations before us. But by the time we become adults, everything we do and who we become are run by our thoughts, belief systems, and internally derived stories. This complex interconnected system also hence dictates what happiness means to us, and what it should look like in a world that runs on a hedonistic definition of happiness. Let me explain.

Close your eyes and meditate on this:

"What is it that makes me really happy right now?"

You might picture smiling faces around you, perhaps happy people and laughing children. You may see yourself standing tall on stage throwing a graduation hat in elation. Some of you may even imagine a yellow Lamborghini, a sprawling mansion and a beautiful wife by your side or some of you may see yourself at the opening of your very own retail outlet, with a line of eager customers outside.

Everyone's definition of happiness is different. But what is common among all of these notions - and here is the caveat – is that happiness is primarily based on what makes us feel good. And for things to feel good, the conditions around us need to fulfil the stories we have created in our mind. For us to be happy, we need to be in pursuit of having good things happen to us, if not occasionally - all the time.

And there is nothing wrong with this line of thinking, because on a rudimentary level, it is true. Feel good, and you will be happy.

> **The issue is - what happens when that good-feeling happy state slips away?** ➤

Unfortunately, no matter how hard we try to hold onto a 'happy state', like all human emotions - the feeling does not last. The problem is that the 'sweet point' fades away just as quickly as it begins. Not only this - waiting for good things to constantly happen to us puts us too much at the mercy of outside circumstances and outside our own locus of control. Like a child chasing after an enchanting firefly, we run after joy and happiness - unaware that it was always within us.

This is how the fruition of "Whole" began. Throughout the book's evolution, it began on the premise that we can obtain a sense of permanent happiness not by being dictated by the conditions that 'happen to us' but rather by what conditions we can cultivate within us. We hear so much about the benefits of modalities such as meditation, mindfulness practices and even psychotherapy and yes - these are definitely powerful ways in enhancing one's sense of well-being. But in our literary world, not much focus is placed on the human virtues we can cultivate in order to fill up that that thirst for a permanent sense of contentment - what I like to refer to as a sense of wholeness. These virtues and self-care techniques are all within our own locus of control and hence, not only do we have the power and capability to practice them, but we can also consciously have fun when we do. Not only this, there is a tremendous amount of cutting-edge neuroscience that backs up the benefits of these tenets, of which you will be privy to later on in the book.

A False Sense of Self

From an early age, most of us have grown into adulthood believing that happiness is derived through our success in school; the number of friends we have; our accolades and achievements in our career; and for many of us our wealth, power and status in society. This conditional belief has evolved over thousands of years, derived from an evolutionary instinct to maintain status quo and be recognised within a group, or to officially belong to a community.

Tracing back our ancestral roots, this desire to belong to a group or tribe would have saved our lives if we were confronted with a tiger lurking behind our backs. However, nowadays the need for a social group in terms of our survival are a lot less of a priority, and instead we rely on society for less trivial things such as approval, validation and reinforcement of our identity. On top of this we have an additional pressure - social media - which only serves to blur the lines of status and symbol even more.

Status and symbol in society have allowed humans to fall even further victim to the whims of the egoistic mind and as a result of this - it seems that we have virtually forgotten our true core nature. What do we mean by this? Our core nature has been described by 'evolved' beings and 'enlightened' masters as a state of pure joy and pure bliss. Simply put, our core nature is the person we were when we had no other attachments other than our primary caregivers. It is the person we were as toddlers and very young children – unaffected and untouched by outside thought and societal conditioning.

Having said this, the present situation is not as grim as it seems. Through diverse social media channels, people are also now openly sharing more personal and uplifting stories of their struggles and revelations as a way to cathartically share their pains and joys. And with these stories also comes an awareness of the importance of self-care and spiritual development. In the same line of thought, there is also a large movement today geared towards becoming a better version of ourselves - towards reaching that state of well-being and joyful awareness. Hence, the demand for self-development programmes and spiritual quests has increased exponentially.

I too, struggled with this. For years, I jumped from one course to another, and constantly scoured through books and programmes on overcoming the self. If I hadn't been careful, I would have become a perpetual "happiness seeker" of sorts. Blindly motivated, I was also determined to help my coaching clients get to their next 'tick' off their list - to take them closer to that 'sweet point'. But as time and experience wore on, it occurred to me that something was fundamentally wrong with this equation. The biggest flaw was the idea that achieving goals and outward based success was the end-goal of life. That expression "light at the end of the tunnel"— it couldn't be farther from the truth.

> It was actually always within our reach - if only we knew how to reach within.

THE ANCIENT DEBATE

Naturally, I wasn't the only one. From the beginning of philosophical and intellectual history, there has been debate on what constitutes "well-being" and "the good life". The controversial turf has since been divided into two branches of thinking, the Hedonic view and the Eudaimonic view[1].

Proposed by the ancient Greek philosopher Aristippus, the Hedonic Approach claims that happiness is derived in terms of attainment of pleasure and avoidance of pain. This school of thought states that the ultimate goal of a human being is to experience the maximum amount of pleasure and that happiness is the culmination of these Hedonic moments. Hobbes wrote in his path-breaking book *Leviathan* that humans are primarily directed by self-interest or "appetites" and that satisfying these appetites assured happiness. DeSade, too, believed that the "pursuit of sensation and pleasure is the ultimate goal of life"[2].

The Eudaimonic Approach, on the other hand, takes the view that hedonic happiness is not the principal criterion of well-being.

Many opponents of the hedonic approach believed pleasure to be a vulgar ideal that enslaved humans to their material desires.

Philosophers such as Aristotle, Socrates and Plato were proponents of the Eudaimonic approach, where realising the true Self or *daimon* was the principal criterion of well-being[3]. Aristotle believed that true happiness may be found in the expression of virtue, that is, in doing what is conducive to human growth and living according to one's authentic values.

A memory of my wedding day crops up as I write this. As my then fiancé and I performed our last round of walking around the fire (the final tradition for becoming man and wife in the Hindu tradition) - the priest sprung a request upon us. We were to recite our marital vows, of which we both were not prepared for. Suddenly put on the spot, my husband paused. He looked down at my hands and then up into my expectant eyes. "I promise to always make her happy". A man of honour and integrity - I really marvelled at the authenticity of his words.

At that point of our lives, did we know what that statement truly entailed? Is happiness and sadness as easy to differentiate as black and white? Or does true happiness come from spinning through the entire spectrum of a convoluted colour wheel? Over the course of a few years, I delved deeply into these two conflicting approaches, searching through endless journals and books on the topic. As time went on, an interesting pattern emerged and out of it culminated this book.

A MORE PERMANENT SENSE OF WELL-BEING

During my research, a term kept springing up in journals – hedonic adaptation. Naturally, it became so important to understand how nothing material or externally derived really makes us happy for very long, nor does it have much real meaning in our lives. Brickman and Campbell called this the "hedonic treadmill", and observed that humans have the tendency to quickly return to a relatively stable level of happiness despite major negative events or life changes.

According to this theory, as a person makes more money, attains more fame, or the like, expectations and desires rise in tandem.

> This simply means that no matter how much money we earn, we will always desire more and more of it.

We will perpetually be stuck in a cycle of wanting and desiring that results in no permanent state of happiness. These ebbs and flows of pleasure are therefore, short-lived.

Personally, after frequent bouts of severe anxiety in my late 20s, a switch in consciousness took over and a desire for more than just "the good life" beckoned me. I wanted to feel not just 'okay' but a more lasting sense of healthy and permanent wellness. This meant I would need something more - a hefty set of tools to keep me grounded. Through reading and studying all sorts of spiritual modalities, one thing became clear; what I was craving within was a sense of deep contentment. Over hell or high water, it became my mission to uncover how I could get there.

Intrigued by the description from mystics and philosophers, I started exploring wholeness from a standpoint of human flourishing. Described by these experts as a feeling of completeness and as a state of consciousness that is full of long-lasting joy - it became clear to me that attaining a sense of wholeness came from a much more grounded sense of reality. If I could come to terms with the idea that no matter what happens around me, no matter what people's opinions may be, or what my outside conditions are - I could feel complete because I was living according to a set of truths that would keep me grounded, stable and content. I wrote this book not because I attained some ordained wisdom and felt obliged to share, but because in my lowest and lost moments I wished I had been able to pick up a how-to book or tool kit to help overcome a struggle; or needed a reminder to take care of my needs; or even learn the secrets of forgiving others, amongst much more. Also, if it had occurred to me earlier that happiness is not a goal with a linear trajectory, but more about the development of a solid character and virtue in the face of hardship - perhaps these truths might have consolidated much sooner.

Learning to Make Peace with Life

Rather than a constant endeavour for ephemeral pleasure, an even more permanent sense of happiness also comes from learning the art of acceptance towards whatever life throws at us. This comes not with resisting pain but learning how to embrace the good with the bad. This is a special art, of course. The art is in developing a conscious awareness that even though life is unjust at times, we should allow all events to unfold organically with minimal resistance. Why?

Because, more often than not, a lot of our misery stems from our resistance of "what is".

In fact, I would totally support the premise that this constant striving for happiness is a deceptive idea—a psychological trap of sorts. What has culminated into a contemporary disease in society has actually led us to fear healthy and formidable challenges. These challenges, whether in the form of pain or sadness may well be worthy of teaching us a lesson on changing our being permanently.

Carl Jung, one of the world's pioneer's in psychoanalysis, hinted at the root cause of this trap. This came across poignantly in a letter to his friend where he noted that alcohol and drug addiction was representative of "the spiritual thirst of our being for wholeness." We are fooled into thinking that we can achieve 'wholeness' by consuming objects of pleasure and hedonistic substances; that it will take us to a happy place. But obviously this is not so.

I have seen the perfect living example of resilience in my mother. A strong-willed woman of worldly wisdom, she was diagnosed two summers ago with Stage 3 Breast Cancer. Having never experienced the chilling threat of cancer in the family, all our worlds were turned upside down and chaos ensued. But little did we all know - we were all in for a wonderful awakening. All throughout the doctor consults, dreary hospital visits, and a series of successful and unsuccessful surgeries - not once did my mother lose her zesty grin and optimistic demeanour. As she continued life 'normally' and with more conviction, she fluidly battled cancer with tenacity and strength of spirit.

According to the doctors, my mother is among the rare 2% who did not endure the full side effects of chemotherapy. She tells me today that her key to recovery was linked to her belief that all that experiential pain really served a greater purpose. If you ask her, she would say the trauma of cancer had led her to become a more instinctive, determined and emotionally resilient human being. I believe one of the main ingredients of this was quite simply because my mother had learnt the art of true acceptance.

It was clear from her wisdom, that life should constitute far more than just a battle for survival - there was much more to it. In fact, although it may not be apparent, life's travails are opportunities for lasting and enriching joy. Of course, there are bound to be bad times, but it is really in our sense of acceptance where we find sanctuary. It is not as easy as it sounds, and hence we will discuss this concept in more detail later on in the book.

KEEPING OUR EMOTIONAL EQUILIBRIUM

The reality is, every day brings a new challenge. And balancing our emotional states so that we don't fly off the handle when excited or sink deep when we feel low is paramount if we are to maintain consistency. We either learn to not live in a perpetual state of sadness or experience it for what it is and move on.

Happiness, like every other emotion, is fleeting. We will be happy, and then we won't. We will be sad, and then we won't. It's that simple.

David Myers writes in his *The Pursuit of Happiness*, "The point cannot be overstated: Every desirable experience—passionate love, a spiritual high, the pleasure of a new possession, the exhilaration of success—is transitory" (1992 p.53)[4]. Quite clearly, happiness and unhappiness are merely short-lived reactions to changes in people's circumstances.

So, what are the secrets to activating this nourishing sense of wholeness? With a combination of strong scientific research and privy to insider stories, 'Whole' ties up 11 distinctive insights on the key to achieving this wholeness of being. My wish is for my valued readers to embrace these insights and come on this eye-opening personal journey with me, not just as a therapist or coach, but also as a mother, wife, daughter, and friend. You will also be going deep into various scientific phenomenon and exploring robust concepts such as the cathartic effect of forgiveness; how our body craves self-care; the difference in modesty and true humility; our misconstrued love for goals; our innate fear of success; the importance of service, and many more.

Each chapter is designed to make it easier for you to navigate through your internal world. Say you are at a standstill or feeling stuck. I want you to be able to open a page in Chapter 6 and learn the secrets of *Self-care*. Or when you feel suddenly overwhelmed, you could easily open Chapter 7 on *Awareness* and learn the trick of slowing down. Or perhaps if you are confused about the concept of helping out others, you could dive into Chapter 9 on the power of *Service*. Also, the interactive structure of the book will help you reach even deeper into your inner self, almost as if you have a coach right in front of you.

The questions and statements highlighted in bold are there for you to close your eyes and meditate on further - really seeking the answers from a place deep within you.

The Summary at the end of each chapter is designed to break everything down for you into a step-by-step guide - which will also help ease you into the concepts further. You might also find yourself looking back at your life and relating your experiences to the lessons at the end of each chapter.

Lastly, before you begin your journey through "Whole", I will leave you with a thought provoking quote by Rune Lazuli "It is not how we live in the light that enlightens us, it is how we live in the dark."[5] And of course, he couldn't be more on point because happiness is not a sudden miracle - it is a slow and gradual evolution.

With deepest gratitude,

Puja

Chapter 1

Willpower
Showing Up For Your Self

"The first and best victory is to conquer the self."
Plato, Greek Philosopher

Reflect back to the last time you caved into a temptation or something you were not really supposed to do. It could have been a few months ago, a year ago or even just yesterday. Thinking back, you might have even said to yourself, "I don't have the willpower to go through with this". We all go through days like this where our defeatist inner dialogue takes over; our willpower wanes, and we feel a looming sense of regret. However, the truth remains steadfast - anyone who has accomplished something worthy in their lives could not have done it without a sturdy sense of self-discipline. The good news is science now backs up the claim that self-discipline is not some divine inborn quality but rather a malleable and learned behaviour. This Chapter taps into the secrets behind developing a strong and steady willpower and also deepens our understanding of why we really do need self-discipline in our lives.

I strongly admire people with unshakable self-discipline. After months of struggling to reach the Yoga Shala in the early hours of the morning, I finally vocalised to my instructor the nature of relentlessly fickle excuses that circled my head every morning.

"Not enough sleep. I'll go tomorrow."

"Body is sore. I'll go tomorrow."

"Long day ahead, need the rest. I'll go tomorrow."

To which he paused, held my shoulder gently and chuckled. I felt silly, like a child as he gently said, "Your excuses don't matter. Whatever you do every morning, just go sit on your yoga mat. Sit on it for however long you want and see where it takes you. That act itself is good enough. Remember it's the commitment of practice that matters. Everything else will fall into place."

Of course, I looked back at him blankly. Who would rightfully wake up at the crack of dawn just to sit on a mat just so that they could *see* where life would take them?

Curious and sceptical, I finally made a decision to heed to his advice. The next morning as I sat sullenly on the mat looking out at the dusky sky, I rolled my eyes as I heard his words echo dimly in my head "…and see where it takes you".

What came next took my breath away. Within five minutes of stillness, my body started to twitch. Suddenly, yearning to move, I found myself starting to fold into the Downward Dog position (the first part of the Ashtanga primary yoga series). With no struggle - it felt so right, and strangely nimble. My body then transitioned into the next *asana* and before I knew it, I was flowing into a practice where time seemed to melt away and my usually resistant self was waning. So, it was true. 'The practice had come', as the wise yogis say.

I did this for almost 42 days consecutively as an experiment. Some days, I woke up, sat on the mat - and earnestly listened to my body's signals. At times, I would be overwhelmed with the need to move into the primary series and the flow of the practice would just take over. And some days, I would sit there, close my eyes, and listen to the birds begin their first chirps as I lay down in the darkness.

As some time passed, an epiphany hit me. It dawned on me that with every act of waking up early I was showing up not for anyone else. Rather, I was showing up for myself - and that was what mattered.

Intuitively it all made so much sense. The practice need not be perfect. It did not have to be long, boring or tiring. Nor did it need not be full of effort. All that was needed was a level of discipline to oneself so that the practice could slowly become engrained. The benefits of this? Huge.

When you are committed to a habit or practice that is virtuous for you in the long-term, the effects start spilling over everywhere. You start suddenly to find changes in your food consumption; sleep patterns; relationships with others; body and most importantly your relishing of life.

REFRAMING HOW WE THINK OF DISCIPLINE

The dictionary definition of 'self-discipline' is the ability to clearly control one's feelings and overcome one's weaknesses. Alas, with a definition so simple, what makes self-discipline such an arduous exercise at times?

In essence, a lot of people shy away from the concept of 'self-discipline' because from early childhood, the term discipline was a common euphemism for "should", "have to", "must", and "need to".

"You **must** brush your teeth every morning."

"You **have to** make your bed before you leave school."

"You **need to** eat your green vegetables if you want to be healthy."

"You **should** study everyday if you want to pass your exams."

It is no wonder that, as adults, we struggle with adding new "shoulds" and "have tos" into our lives! This dilemma is further aggravated because on a biological level humans have a natural tendency to resist being "forced" into situations.

In fact, our brains hate it.

Not to be taken lightly, there is a psychological phenomenon known as reactance in which a person has a negative reaction when being forced or persuaded to do something. When feeling obliged to commit to a change in our lifestyles, we feel our freedom of choice is being controlled - and often end up doing exactly what we are advocated against.

On the other hand, imagine if an entire topic on self-discipline became a dedicated subject in school. If this was the case, as small children we would learn that maintaining a healthy sense of self-discipline is not just imperative for achieving small daily successes but in fact is also a huge contribution towards the health of our mind and body.

With regards to a healthy mind, when we have the fortitude to stick to a discipline or a habit that we have committed ourselves to - we are in reality acting out of integrity to ourselves.

> And if we have a firm belief in our ability to remain consistent, our 'inner' and 'outer' worlds can finally synchronise, and we can experience a satisfying congruency within.

I felt this sense of congruency deep within my bones as I chose to stick to a low carb lifestyle of eating for a few months. But the true test of willpower took place when we visited Paris and Rome for the Easter break. Not touching croissants, pastries, macaroons and the deserts, which my family mulled over, was best described as agony. But I had learned my lesson before - if I dared to cheat - I knew I would be overcome with a sense of self-betrayal. And having suffered from weight issues since the birth of my children, I was determined. With a clear goal in mind, and enough practice of being on the low carb bandwagon - my resistance to sugar was much easier. All I had to do was manage my moods and make sure that I would not pick up the wrong food in a state of being hungry or tired. Despite the temptation, I had matched my inner desires with my outer actions - and had proved to myself I could do what I set my mind to do.

When we engage in healthy habits for our bodies, so much good stuff happens besides increasing our longevity, heart health and our energy levels. Let's look at this.

Do you sometimes wonder why you feel so great after a workout? It's not just the thousands of endorphins pervading our blood. I attribute half that sense of "great feeling" to the accomplishment of the fact that I even showed up in the first place. Compare this sense of accomplishment with the guilt you might feel at missing a personal training session. We have all felt that regret when we skip out on a commitment or do a no-show.

So, in a sense, being disciplined with ourselves is a gateway to feeling better within ourselves. When we stick to what we say we will do, it is extremely satisfying because distractions can come and go; temptations might sneak right up under our noses; but our moral conviction and resolve does not let that come in the way. This mere act reaffirms the faith that we have in ourselves.

> Contrary to what most people might believe, there is great freedom in the act of self-discipline, as we finally become released from being a slave to our desires.

If you think about it, do you ever question the small, internalised disciplines you have developed, such as brushing your teeth or taking a shower? Hardly anyone ever questions these things, because we were conditioned at an early age to believe that these were things we must do. As a result of time and regularity, these habits have become so automatic to our lives we do not question them at all.

So, the willpower dilemma really only arises at the beginning of our early adult lives, when we are able to set self-imposed disciplines for ourselves. What are some examples of self-imposed disciplines? A lot of self-disciplines are actually acts of self-care and conducive habits that propel us towards our goals. Of course, everyone's versions differ from each other.

Anne's version of self-care is beginning her day at 5am. This is so she can fit in a meditation and journaling regime before she gets the kids lunchboxes ready and heads off to work.

Priscilla has set up a disciplined regime of sticking to two cups of coffee per day as she has a history of anxiety and panic attacks.

You might catch Ahmed in his office cabin doing breathing exercises while on an empty stomach before lunch. He purposely times this to help him cut food cravings, as he has been suffering with obesity for over decades.

Naturally, everyone has their own version of self-care and self-discipline.

There are those amongst us who set up ambitious disciplines for ourselves, but just can't follow through or maintain some level of consistency. Either our willpower, the backbone of discipline, gets depleted and we cave into temptation; or we yield into procrastination, implementing the "leave it for tomorrow" strategy.

And there are those of us lucky ones whose disciplines become so infused into our lives, that those disciplines become habits and our bedrock of routine - to the point that we have even forgotten we have set them up in the first place.

Now that we have looked at some examples of self-imposed disciplines, it might be useful for you to consider what type of habits you have created in your life that match your health and mental well-being.

> The challenge is then, unlocking the tools which help keep us motivated and consistent.

But in order to do this, it is important to recognise the biggest thing that stands in our way - our brains.

How Does the Brain Handle Temptation?

Oscar Wilde was really onto something when he said, "I can resist everything except temptation." For discipline to be healthily engrained into our daily lives, one needs to learn how to eventually master a strong level of willpower. But in order to achieve this type of mental strength, we must first understand the science behind a peculiar phenomenon, and how it can actually work to our advantage. In fact, research conducted by Roy Baumeister of Florida State University, (an expert on mental strength), puts forth that exerting self-control requires great effort.

> In a metaphorical sense, one could imagine willpower like a battery. The aim of the battery, of course, is to provide an electrical current or energy towards an object.

But a battery's downfall is that it also has a limited lifespan and it is eventually going to run out. Through a series of studies, Baumeister demonstrates that self-control is actually similar to a battery. And if we over-exert our self-control battery, it eventually leads to something known as 'ego depletion'. During ego depletion, our willpower, (by acting like another entity in itself) goes through three stages. Its strength diminishes and begins to fade; it starts to backfire, and then eventually physically fatigues us.

Back in the 90s, Roy Baumeister conducted an experiment where he examined the effects of a tempting food experiment. This challenge was designed to deplete the participants' willpower.

The Chocolate and Radish Experiment

In the first part of the experiment, Baumeister kept a group of approximately 67 college students in a room that smelled of freshly baked chocolate cookies and then proceeded to show them the actual treats. However, a number of participants were asked to eat radishes instead while the rest could indulge in the cookies. As the scientists observed in their published paper two years later, many of the radish-eaters "exhibited clear interest in the chocolates, to the point of looking longingly at the chocolate display and in a few cases even picking up the cookies to sniff at them."[6]

Immediately following this, Baumeister's team gave the participants an extremely difficult puzzle to solve. The rule was that you had to eat the food before attempting the puzzle. What the studies showed was that the students who ate the radishes gave up on the puzzle after an average of eight minutes. However, the cookie group persisted about twice as long. The radish-eaters exercised exerting self-control in eating something unpleasant, thereby depleting their willpower reserves and were experiencing ego depletion.[7]

In the world of psychology and behavioural science, this seemingly simple study was a huge breakthrough. The key findings show that if we would like our willpower to remain consistently strong throughout the day, we clearly need to strategise how we structure our everyday activities. If we do this wisely, there is also no temptation towards decision fatigue. What is even more compelling throughout all of Baumeister's research is this:

Self-control is strongest in the morning but progressively wears out as the day goes on. ⮞

Anything that takes too much mental energy away from ourselves: like a stressful day at work; the pressure to resist carbohydrates for breakfast and lunch; or even controlling our emotions with a difficult boss - can actually work against us by the end of the night. And because of the nature of ego depletion, we are more at risk of waning towards making bad decisions, losing our temper or caving into something unhealthy at the end of the day. Hence, how we structure our day has enormous implications on our self-control muscle, especially if we want to stick to a discipline or create new habits.

With these findings, it is no more a mystery as to why we find it easier to stick to our diets early in the morning, but as the day wears on we find ourselves losing ourselves to temptation or laziness.

In a way, the act of self-control is similar to the functioning of a muscle that is constantly moving - once it tires and can no longer perform at peak strength, the muscle eventually just gives in. On the same trajectory, it is also a 'brain drain' and erodes the power to focus and do other deep work.

Now, we may not be acutely aware of this but when we put on a social mask or pretend to be something we are not - a certain amount of self-control is exhausted. This also then weakens our will-power 'muscle' later on in the day. To cite an example, research shows that the little fib you told your friend at the supermarket is not so good for your ability to focus during for the rest of the day. Let's say you convey to your friend about how you are doing fine, (even though you could be in the midst of a crisis). The science shows that this seemingly small and insignificant act will genuinely create a feeling of discomfort and incongruence within you and hence actually make it harder for you to focus later on. What this means is an attempt to hide who you really, or how you are really feeling does a few detrimental things to you. It is shown to deplete the energy that is needed to control your emotions; your ability to engage deeply and efficiently in a task; and it might even cause you to react more aggressively to another provocation. On the other hand, when we are completely honest about how we feel or what we mean, a whole burden is lifted for us- and hence we can focus better. So, even something as simple as maintaining transparency and honesty in our lives affects our level of self-control.

A lot of us tend to put challenging things off to the last minute where our running background reel that says "I don't feel like it" ends up taking precedence over our goals.

Procrastination refers to the "voluntary postponement of an unpleasant task, often against one's better judgement"[8]. As tempting as it may be to postpone things for the future, it simply does not do us much good. When we have the habit of leaving things to the last minute with our backs against the wall, not only does it manifest itself through a sub-standard quality of work, but it also results in a reduced sense of well-being.

Many psychologists have attempted to understand the causes of procrastination. In fact, Sigmund Freud even went so far as to relate this behaviour to issues that stem from poor toilet training during childhood.[9] Being that there is a multitude of research and literature on 'procrastination', I'd like to simplify it here.

At this point, the most important thing is for us to recognise are the core psychological triggers which cause humans to procrastinate. For those of us who like to leave things to the last moment, at least we are not fighting a battle against ourselves that we have no knowledge of. So, here are a few of them stated below, and you might actually find you can identify with one- if not more.

- *Our Fear of Failure*
  One of the strongest indicators towards procrastination is the fear of making a mistake or of not doing something "good enough". When putting effort into a task or project is necessary, but the thought of doing something wrong or looking foolish makes you panic- this is a sign you could be avoiding 'failure'. The fear of making a mistake in the public eye or even to ourselves sometimes leads us to feel ashamed- and hence, we choose avoidance tactics, (and one of these is procrastination).

- ## *Our Fear of Achievement*
  Procrastination is also a metaphorical tool that shields people from larger expectations and greater obligations. This can be best described as the 'side-effects' that may follow success - such as fame or a sudden personal accountability to others. Similar to those who procrastinate out of their fear of failure or making a mistake, in this context one keeps themselves protected from a bigger responsibility (as a result of great achievements).

- ## *Not Enough Structure in the Task*
  Sometimes tasks and activities frighten us because perhaps they appear to be large in scope or challenging in nature. What is really going on here, however, is that we have not mastered the ability to break down the task into small, digestible and do-able steps. A solution to this would be to schedule a step-by-step itinerary and to input it into our calendars. Not only then does the task become clearer and easier to handle, but there is more joy in tackling each task one by one because humans thrive working with a manageable structure. It is no wonder then that having a clear agenda is the key to mastering a sense of self-discipline. In a way, we are going easy on ourselves when we break a big task down into digestible parts.

- ## *Not Enough Belief in our Abilities*
  Of course, there are days when we tend to doubt ourselves and own abilities to undertake even the simplest of tasks. When we go through low times, sometimes we find that our self-confidence is thwarted and we start succumbing to all sorts of limiting beliefs. A limiting belief occurs when we are operating from our past conditions or experiences. Some limiting beliefs are created during childhood whilst learning from our respected elders. As an 8-year-old child, my exasperated Math teacher in England only just once snapped, "Oh you'll never be good at Maths anyway, so don't bother!" As a consequence, every future attempt to solve a mathematical equation would be filled with dread and doubt, which ended up seriously thwarting my confidence levels in Maths. From time to time, I can still hear

her voice ringing in my head every time I see a mathematical equation in my daughter's workbook.

On the other hand, perhaps you are having a bad day at work and a low feeling infiltrates into your every move, further demotivating you to carry out a task. A sudden burst of low confidence thwarts you from doing what you said you would do.

Thankfully, we have the ability to switch this around.

> Studies have shown that those with a strong belief in their abilities are more likely to continue their efforts with whatever task they have set themselves up to do.

Personally, when I find myself in a slump and feeling demotivated- I remind myself that whatever I set out to do is "better done than perfect". Just taking the effort to try and is good enough, and the task definitely does not need to be perfect - not for anyone, and not for myself. Because my need for consistency was so strong, I created this mantra for my work desk:

'What I do does not define me, but what does is my commitment and consistency to carry it out.'

After all, there is a special feeling of pride in knowing that you would stick to what you said you will do, despite what is going on around you.

• *Not Enough 'Why' in You.*
As Jim Rohn, a well-known American motivation expert poignantly says, "When the why is clear, the how is easy".

Not thinking back to the reason we began the task in the first place is a huge deterrent to finishing through.

> Because our brain craves novel and enriching experiences, (especially at the beginning stages of any new task) our motivation levels usually start with a robust high.

However, without the constant reminder of a long-term reward, gain or a clear purpose ('why'), we naturally and inevitably lose momentum.

When I find myself slipping away from a beneficial habit or commitment, I use a simple NLP technique to get back me on track.

I close my eyes and reflect back to where I am going to be once I have achieved my task or finished a project. Visually, I imagine where I will be standing or sitting; what I will be wearing; and perhaps the expression on my face. Then I imagine what I will hear around me or the sounds of the place I am in. Lastly, I will allow myself to relish the satisfying or elated emotions that would be coursing through my body once I have achieved what I wanted in the first place. Suddenly, the end-goal all becomes real to me again, and I am reminded and aligned to why I started in the first place.

Our brains need constant reminders for why we do the things we do. That is why imagining and believing in future results help re-calibrate our 'why'. So, it would be a wise move to go back here every time you find yourself stuck in completing a task.

Your Best Kept Secrets to Getting Things Done

Consistent self-discipline can organically turn into automatic behaviours of everyday living. But first, how do we avoid the phenomenon of ego depletion that occurs when our willpower wanes? And what are some tools to help us resist the temptation to procrastinate?

> Good habits and disciplines are best linked to goals which attain a particular inward state, also known as an intrinsic reward.

An example of this would be linking our results to a valuable internal outcome. A clear and ready example of this would be attending a weight loss retreat in order to improve one's long-term health, as opposed to conforming to the needs of society's idea of what thin or fat is.

As motivating as it is to gain the admiration of others around you, the fact is attention-seeking and external validation is less sustainable for our goals in the long term. However, if the motivating factor is related to an inward state- such as achieving optimum health- it is inevitable that the goal ends up becoming an integral part of everything you do. Hence, your disciplines should be closely linked to what is really important for you, your family and your well-being.

> For disciplines to take hold, consistency is paramount.

Aristotle very rightly pointed out more than a thousand years ago, that we are a product of what we repeatedly do. For so many years however, I struggled. I would start things - projects, exercise regimes, diets, online courses - and give it up within months, either out of sheer boredom or lack of motivation. And I am sure, I'm definitely not alone here.

We all know that forming lifelong habits need considerable effort but understanding the chemistry of our brain also plays a large role in sticking to a disciplined lifestyle.

> A psychological phenomenon known as synaptic pruning demonstrates that as adults, we build our strengths with the things we do frequently.

You might have even heard of the famous quote by Donald Hebb, a Canadian Neuropsychologist: "Neurons that fire together wire together".

This is because the more we practice a skill or discipline- the stronger, thicker and more efficient the connection forms between the neurons in our brain. Hence, staying committed to a habit becomes easier and more automatic. In fact, there are several theories claiming that it takes approximately 21-30 days to integrate a habit into our everyday lives. Deanne Ware, Ph.D., in Neuropsychology writes it best on her blog:

"Our brain cells communicate with one another via synaptic transmission–one brain cell releases a chemical (neurotransmitter) that the next brain cell absorbs. This communication process is known as "neuronal firing." When brain cells communicate frequently, the connection between them strengthens. Messages that travel the same pathway in the brain over & over begin to transmit faster & faster. With enough repetition, they become automatic. That's why we practice things like hitting a golf ball–with enough practice, we can go on automatic pilot."[10]

Categorising your Tasks. A major source of stress in our lives comes from the overwhelm of having an incredibly long list of things to complete. The stress could also be attributed to the idea that projects are unattainable because they are so 'complex' or 'vast' in nature- and you simply just do not know where to begin.

Say for example, you are writing a book. At the conceptual level, you have a somewhat concrete vision for the book. However, because you have so much content reeling around your head, you just do not know how and where to start penning it all down. In this kind of scenario, it would be wise by beginning to break your concepts into smaller digestible nuggets of information.

Perhaps you might want to create a vision board. Under the vision board you can have bullet points of the main ideas you would like to bring out in your book. Once you have done this, you can create a bullet point list of all the topics relating to your ideas- and these eventually become the titles of your book chapters. Now, that you now are able to clearly pinpoint the outline of your book, next to every chapter you could allocate a reasonable date to complete each one by. This timeline could be shared with someone accountable, who has some vested interest in your success or is a mentor.

'The Chain Method'. Although some might say the secret to success is to work hard and to put in long arduous hours, I find it is quite the opposite. While writing this book, I limited my day to a 2-hour writing schedule or simply until my laptop battery would conk out. Nothing less or beyond that. Nine days out of twelve, I would be staring at my computer blankly – unable to weave the words that I so desperately wanted to type out. So, I would sit until my 2-hour slot was over, knowing intuitively the words would start flowing. Patience was key, if I were to maintain this level of consistency.

The key to success, in my experience, is keeping the mind-set of 'progress, not perfection' strong at the forefront of our thinking. Even little steps in the right direction is good enough, as long as you remain consistent in your actions. In fact, Cal Newport in his book "Deep Work" mentions a concept known as the chain method.

"This philosophy argues that the easiest way to consistently start deep work sessions is to transform them into a simple regular habit. The goal is to generate a rhythm for this work that removes the need for you to invest energy in deciding if and when you're going to go deep."[11]

Mini Breaks to Avoid Ego Depletion.

Research now points to the fact that the brain is only able to maintain intense focus for around 45 minutes before it loses momentum.

Hence, the idea is to take as many small breaks through the day, enriched with refreshing intervals that help boost your brainpower and attention levels. If your discipline is to complete a 300-page thesis, it may be advisable to get up frequently and go for quick 5-minute walks around the courtyard. As Nietzsche said, "It is only ideas gained from walking that have any worth."

Some quick activities in-between the major tasks, help. Having a quick laugh with a colleague in between a heavy meeting at work, or making a quick run up the stairs if you are feeling lethargic are just some examples of mini-breaks you can give yourself. The point is - don't stress about the way you take your break- just choose a varied activity every hour or so.

Meditation helps improve self-control. There is a considerable amount of scientific evidence to support the fact that having a long-term meditation practice helps decrease our cravings and hence helps increase our self-control.

You might wonder, but how?

In a 2009 Duke University-Caltech study, scientists analysed the brains of 37 dieters while they looked at photos of fifty different food items. The findings showed that the "dorsolateral prefrontal cortex" (which is the part of the brain that was activated by people with higher levels of willpower) is the same area of the brain which is highly active during meditation.

Hence, the more you engage in meditative practices- the more you end up strengthening this part of your prefrontal cortex, largely responsible for willpower. This naturally then lends to a healthier sense of self-discipline.

Establish an Accountability Partner. I am pretty sure my editor thought I was 'jumping the gun' by signing the publishing contract long before I was even through with my third chapter for this book. However, I did eventually convince her that there was a method behind the madness. Not only did I need motivation, a structure and deadlines so I could remain consistent with my writing, but I also really needed an accountability partner. I had learned the hard way years ago: starting super motivated, taking a break halfway, procrastinating and then eventually resigning on the task. This time I was so sure that the key to having someone silently 'holding my hand', was also the secret to keep me on track and help me finish this book.

> Just like Weight Watchers, Alcoholics Anonymous, Mastermind Groups all come together to provide support to individuals - this social magnet phenomenon makes people more likely to stay focused and accomplish tasks.

Quite simply, it is because as humans we feel an accountability towards our 'tribes' or groups we are part of and feel a need to remain consistent with our word. Having an accountability partner addresses a human need to feel encouraged and empowered.

The author of "Deep Work", Cal Newport, wraps it up poignantly:

"This back and forth represents a collaborative form of deep work that leverages what I call the whiteboard effect. For some types of problems, working with someone else at the proverbial shared whiteboard can push you deeper than if you were working alone. The presence of the other party waiting for your next insight- be it someone physically in the same room or collaborating with you virtually - can short circuit the natural instinct to avoid depth."[12]

SUMMARY
The act of self-discipline is more than just achieving goals or working towards something important, (although it forms a large part). Just as important, however, is that it also gifts us the power of congruence - of being in integrity to what we said we would do. So, what are some key secrets to working towards a healthy sense of self-discipline?

- **Link your discipline to an inward state, rather than an outside reward.** An example of this would be to reframe how you think about something. For example, for someone wanting to lose weight, instead of the mind-set, "I want to look good so people can notice me", you might want to reframe:

  "I want to remain healthy and fit, so I can feel lighter and full of energy. When I am lighter and have higher energy levels, I can live a better life."

- **Consistency is Paramount.** The idea is to just keep chipping away so the habit or discipline becomes part of your everyday life. (Even if it means for only 5 minutes a day.) The idea is to engrain the practice into your system, just like waking up and brushing your teeth.

- **Chunk your Tasks Down.** If you have a big project and are suddenly feeling overwhelmed, break the project down into mini-actions and set it against a reasonable timeline. Sit down every day and tackle just those few tasks. Then, leave the rest. This, in itself, is also an act of discipline as you commit yourself to only those actions that you set yourself out to do.

- **The "Chain Method".** The easiest way to consistently start deep work sessions is to transform them into a simple regular habit.

- **Mini Breaks to Avoid 'Ego Depletion'.** Because we are only able to maintain intense focus for around 45 minutes, a refreshing quick break every hour is invigorating and essential.

- **Meditation helps develop Willpower.** The section of the brain activated by people with high levels of willpower is the same area of the brain which is highly active during meditation. Hence, meditation helps in strengthening the discipline muscle.

- **Establish an Accountability Partner.** The social magnet phenomenon makes people more likely to maintain self-discipline and accomplish tasks because they feel accountable to another person or group.

CHAPTER 2

CREATIVITY
LEADING YOU TOWARDS BREAKTHROUGH

I think 99 times and I find nothing. I stop thinking, swim in silence,
and the truth comes to me.
Albert Einstein

There is no deeper internal fulfillment within than when we are living from
real and authentically inspired action. And the secret towards our most inspired
'Aha!' moments, breakthroughs and soundest decisions are all actually linked
to how best our brains work when presented with certain conditions. But
the challenge is - how do we remain fresh and inspired amidst a life that is
constantly in motion? More often than not, we find ourselves living on overdrive
- otherwise known as survival mode. If we are not bottlenecked with to-do lists,
emails, social media notifications - we are also dealing with out-of-town guests,
social obligations, frequent travel schedules, and stringent work deadlines. No
wonder we are highly susceptible to distraction and end up just about winging
important tasks. This Chapter explores under the internal and environmental
conditions our brain requires in order to remain fresh and inspired. You will
also be reading on how stress blocks our creative capacities and a reduced power
to perform tasks. Lastly, there are some practical tips to channel oneself into a
'flow' mode, also known as 'being in the zone'.

Staring emptily at a white and expressionless Microsoft Word
document, waiting for some epiphany to hit - I paradoxically
reflect on what interesting times we are living in. Here we are in

an age of such deep technological advancement, that even our brains can be measured down to how and when we get our deepest inspiration and insights.

Of all the numerous insights brain MRI scans that have now brought us, one of the biggest discoveries has been this.

> Our most profound moments of inspired action occur not at a level when we are intensely focused on one idea - but in fact at a level when our brains are in a relaxed, restful state of mind. 🌱

To quote Brigid Schulte, author of *Overwhelmed: Work, Love, and Play When No One Has the Time*: "Scientists have found that people who take time to daydream score higher on tests of creativity. When our brains are idle, the default mode network lights up, connecting parts of our brain that don't typically communicate when we're focused on a task. So a random thought, a stray memory, the snippet of a song, a dream fragment can all combine in a fresh way and produce an entirely new idea."[13]

Whilst writing "Whole", I hit several metaphorical walls, characterised by listless sessions of mind wandering and intense daydreaming. At times a blank screen became my best friend and other times - my nemesis. (Some might label this phenomenon as 'writers block', but I describe these bouts more dramatically as 'brain coma'.)

And sometimes, these blank gaps lasted weeks - relentlessly postponing my goals. What I didn't realise, though, was that these gaps of so-called wasted clock time actually gifted my mind something special. What had appeared to be listless wondering and empty white pages, actually provided me with the space, time and energy to map out crucial aspects of the book. Those days of 'nothing' allowed my mind to further reflect on the material even deeper, to the point where suddenly relevant situations and stories started to pop up which synchronistically tied in with whatever I was writing at that point. In fact, those days of listlessness provided for more interesting depictions for each Chapter and hence, more vivid content creation.

How did I know this to be true?

I would be walking along the beach, and a past memory relevant to the topic on "courage" would arise. Or a few brief peaceful moments of silence with my son while putting him to sleep, would inspire an idea for the reading on "integrity". Even just sitting solo on a park bench - passively aware of a lonely swan dip in and out of the lake - would stir up conceptual intimacies for the chapter on "self-awareness". All this would have never occurred to me while staring frustratingly at a digital white screen. Words, images, concepts, interweaved metaphors, life examples - all of these things would start connecting, one by one - like pieces of a puzzle coming together. The Chapter would finally come to life, if I just allowed myself to 'let go' and become present with what was around me.

Pico Iyer, one of the greatest writers of our time has spent more than 30 years tracking movement and stillness. To access his "deepest voice" and gain inspiration for his writing, Iyer has visited the Benedictine hermitage over 80 times in the past 24 years, even though he says he does not follow any particular religion. He says:

"When I go to my monastery in Big Sur, I spend a lot of time doing nothing, taking walks, lying on my bed—and I'm confident that it's only in that space that I will come up with something fresh and more interesting than my everyday ideas…As soon as I am in stillness, I can hear my deepest voice, everything that becomes inaudible when I am in constant motion."[14]

So, if creative inspiration is largely spurred by a relaxed mind - what the science is really telling us is that being in a state of constant motion and overdrive (of which so many of us are in) actually ends up obstructing our creativity. Let's explore this more. But before we do that, let us first unbury and break down what we mean by 'creativity'.

LIVING IN A STATE OF CREATION, AND NOT SURVIVAL

When we speak of creativity, we are not only referring to the conventional conception of creating art, music, dance, poems, novels, sculptures and other such manifestations. We are also referring to a type of inspired action that drives humans towards focused and deep thinking; inspirational visions (also driven by intuition and gut feelings); 'aha' moments and wise decisions - all of which drive successful outcomes.

On a spiritual level, it would be worth pointing out that to live in a state of creation is to also live with a certain kind of freedom.

> **What this means is that through creative human expression we are able to unconsciously release 'age-old blockages', stagnant or heavy energies, and built-up emotions.**

No one of course says it better than the great Indian spiritual master, Osho, in his book *Creativity: Unleashing the Forces Within*:

> "The creative person is one who brings something from the unknown into the world of the known, who brings something from God into the world, who helps God to utter something—who becomes a hollow bamboo and allows God to flow through him. How can you become a hollow bamboo? If you are too full of the mind, you cannot become a hollow bamboo. And creativity is from the creator, creativity is not of you or from you. You disappear, then creativity is—when the creator takes possession of you."[15]

Now, the opposite of living in a creative state of being is living in something known as survival mode. Survival mode is when we are struggling to make it through even the simplest of days.

Here, one can imagine a person running from meeting to meeting, unfocused, uninspired and living in a state of flux. Tunnel-visioned and stressed, when we are in survival mode, we are not living in true synchronicity with what we aspire to see and create. As a result, the answers we seek do not come to us in inspiration but instead - in desperation (marred by stress). It is no wonder our solutions to problems end up, run-of-the-mill and mediocre. And then we wrongly blame it on our busy life.

Do you sometimes find yourself blank when it comes to facing an actually simple problem?

Or perhaps you look at your to-do list and you experience a sense of anxiety and overwhelm?

Or do you, at times, rely on others to make decisions for you, even for the smallest things?

These are all common symptoms of living in overdrive mode. In fact, at times, the anxiety of not being able to deal with the simplest of things causes us to even snap at others out of frustration. We might even find our short-term memory failing us. Some live in a state of bewilderment where the smallest things appear so daunting in their minds, that they cannot even fathom the thought of leaving their home. Once in a while, a client will come to me and say, "Even the small things seem really big in my head and I can't seem to do it." In a sense, we feel like we have been drained dry and our supply of inspiration has been exhausted. Feeling alive and inspired feels like a far-away dream. And then we wonder — how did we even get to this place?

LIVING IN A STATE OF OVERDRIVE: SURVIVAL MODE

Society's stress levels are at an all-time high. Globally, more than 300 million people suffer from depression, and 260 million suffer from anxiety disorders many of whom just live with both conditions.[16] A study by the World Health Organization found that such disorders cost the global economy $1 trillion in lost productivity each year.[17] On top of this, around two billion residents of our planet are online with the average person spending 25 hours online a week.[18] It is no wonder that stress levels are soaring rocket high and anxiety disorders are the most common mental illness affecting 40 million adults in the United States.[19]

Not only is the pace of life more demanding, but unlike in the past, our minds have now also become trained to constantly check our devices and inboxes every few minutes. According to a recent article,

'Smartphone users have developed what they call "checking habits" - repetitive checks of e-mail and other applications such as Facebook. The checks typically lasted less than 30 seconds and were often done within 10 minutes of each other. On average, the study subjects checked their phones 34 times a day, not necessarily because they really needed to check them that many times, but because it had become a habit or compulsion.'[20]

I am sure you have experienced that sweet split second when you were finally 'onto something' or you recalled an important piece of information and then your phone goes 'buzz'. Boom - you've lost your flow. On top of this, with all the new influx of data, you now have more information to think about and 'upload'.

The majority of us holding onto a smartphone are hooked to an endless source of infotainment from sources like Twitter, Facebook, Pinterest and the like. This constant bombardment of information (in addition to the requirements of our family, jobs and social obligations) leaves us in a constant state of activity - where our minds are constantly working and not able to get any downtime. I am convinced that if a neuroscientist were to attach nodes to our brains throughout the day, the brainwaves would show consistently high levels of 'beta activity'. Being in a state of beta indicates a heightened state of alertness, logic and critical reasoning. However, our brains are not built to stay in beta mode the whole day, and it is hence no wonder this generation of smartphone users are so emotionally and mentally zapped by the time their heads hit the pillow. The oversupply of information and increased stimulation simply leaves no time for our brains to settle down; process the day; link thoughts and meanings together; and most importantly - create.

> There is no better way of saying it: overstimulation equals stress and stress equals to low creativity.

THE SCIENCE: STRESS & LOW INSPIRATION

Looking at our body's biochemistry, how do moments of stress affect our brains? Let's say you receive a sudden email from your boss requesting you to come to his cabin 'asap'. What happens to your brain and body at that moment?

> Because the nature of our subconscious mind is not equipped to distinguish between 'real' and 'perceived' danger (such as a truck bounding meters towards you vs. an argument with our spouse), our fight-or-flight response automatically gets triggered.

When this happens, our body is flooded with hormones as if on mode to save our lives.

The most ancient and primitive part of the brain known as the hypothalamus, reacts to this perceived danger by sending a signal to the organs to release adrenalin. When this happens, the body reacts by quickening the heart rate, speeding the breath and preparing us to either fight or run away. While all this is going on, the brain reallocates resources to this primitive part of the brain and away from our command centre, that is, the prefrontal cortex (PFC). The PFC — evolutionarily the newest part of our brain — is responsible for higher cognitive functions, such as creativity, rationalisation, abstract thinking and logic. But under great stress the brain is fooled into thinking the body is under real threat, and can hence reallocates energy from the Prefrontal Cortex to the primal part of the brain. Because of the perceived danger, the brain prioritises primal emotions over abstract thinking and motor control over creativity.

This simply means that rationality goes out the window, and our brains prepare our body to go into fight mode.

No wonder, neurologically speaking, when we are under great stress our brain reacts by locking us out of the creative part of the brain. It is not the brain's fault though. If you think about it, diverting these resources are the brain's way of finding the quickest shortcut to save our lives. But life can also take a turn for the worst when we are operating with this certain kind of tunnel-vision: for example, we might even lash out at others without thinking about the long-term consequences.

This also explains why in times of stress, our thought processes become skewed and we make wrong decisions.

Moreover, a study conducted by John Morrison from The Mount Sinai School of Medicine, has found that prefrontal dendrites in the prefrontal cortex (the branches of a neuron) are affected by stress. And while they could regrow if stress disappears, they cannot rebound after chronic stress. In other words, if we are exposed to constant stressful situations, and remain in this highly aroused state, our prefrontal function responsible for deep thinking weakens. [21]

WHY ARE SO WE CONCERNED WITH BEING IN A STATE OF FLOW?
What a paradox it is that stress and anxiety hampers creativity - yet if you were to turn the turtle on its back - it is quite the opposite.

In fact, engaging in creative activities and being in a 'state of flow' actually helps decrease stress.

A US-based study focused on creativity found that college students who completed creative projects experienced a decrease in anxiety compared to those who didn't. This is because when we partake in creative activities we are engaged in what experts describe as a sense of 'flow'. As psychologist Elaine Slater explains:

"This can put us in a near-meditative state where we lose track of time and feel removed from the stressors of life."

'Flow' is a term coined by Psychologist Mihaly Csikszentmihalyi and has become a well-known concept in the field of positive psychology. It is what you would have heard about as being in 'the zone'. This occurs when one is so fully immersed in an activity, that he or she actually loses their sense of space and time. Csikszentmihalyi – who coined the term 'Flow' – argues that our best moments occur when we create and invoke our imaginations: "The best moments usually occur when a person's body or mind is stretched to its limits in a voluntary effort to accomplish something difficult and worthwhile. Optimal experience is thus something that we make happen."[22]

(Admittedly, I struggle with Csikszentmihalyi's interpretation of 'difficult', and prefer approaching the effort directed towards a task as 'engaging' instead.)

You must have heard the expression: "time flies when you are having fun." A similar phenomenon occurs when you 'lose yourself' in the creative composition of a song, walking through a lush forest, or something even as simple as folding an origami giraffe. When you are lucky enough to experience this sense of 'flow', you are so aware of what you are doing because all your five senses are fully engaged and no outside distraction can disturb you. You experience a state where you have lost track of what is perceived to be 'clock time' and hence in spiritual terms, you lose a little bit of your egoist sense of self.

We might have read about the wonders of 'being present' and the benefits of having all of our senses engaged in whatever task we are doing.

> **And there is scientific evidence to show that in this state of perceived aliveness - this is where the real magic happens.**

This is the time when our thoughts and decisions operate at its highest frequency and true inspiration lies.

It all sounds too good to be true. So, from a scientific perspective how and why does this happen? Steven Kotler, co-founder of the Flow Genome Project (an organization dedicated to flow state research) writes, "During flow, the brain releases an enormous cascade of neurochemistry. Large quantities of norepinephrine, dopamine, endorphins, anandamide, and serotonin flood our system. All are pleasure-inducing, performance-enhancing chemicals with considerable impacts on creativity. Both norepinephrine and dopamine amp up focus, boosting imaginative possibilities by helping us gather more information. They also lower signal-to-noise ratios, increasing pattern recognition or our ability to link ideas together in new ways. Anandamide, meanwhile, increases lateral thinking—meaning it expands the size of the database searched by the pattern recognition system."[23]

CREATIVITY BEGETS CREATIVITY

What is even more fascinating in this area of research is that even a small trace of creativity leads to an increase of creativity in other areas. Why? This is because being actively imaginative helps us gain confidence in our own abilities. When we are more confident in our abilities, we are hence motivated to think more creatively in other aspects of our life, be it at the office, at home or even at the bar (wink)!

More good news.

Not only do we gain confidence and self-esteem, but another study conducted on 1,000 elderly men, undertaken by Nicolas Turiano - shows that creativity is actually unrelated to age. The study proves that "creative people tend to handle stress better as they reframe potential obstacles".

In addition to this, they found that individuals who engaged in creative tasks lived markedly longer, presumably because the very act of creation stimulates many regions in the brain which keeps the brain healthier. Nicolas's studies confirm that

"Creativity not only can potentially enable people of any age to adapt better to life circumstances, but also has particular salience for older adults. It may confer on them an ability to better confront the problems associated with increasing age and declining health, and may have important effects on slowing cognitive aging."[24]

This is good news for the elderly as the very act of creation stimulates many regions that keeps the brain healthy. Hence, we should be encouraging our elders to become more engaged in music, drawing, painting or any other such creative endeavours so as to keep their brains engaged and healthy. As my grandmother approached early stages of dementia, I instinctively knew that enhancing her favourite tic-tac-toe skills and origami folding would keep her cognitively afloat - at least until the disease really kicked in.

MOVING TOWARDS ALPHA: HOW A RELAXED BRAIN FUELS BREAKTHROUGH SUCCESS

Long before the science even amassed, reaching that sweet spot of inspired action is something prosperous people have been grasping towards for centuries. For instance, Charles Darwin took exceptionally long walks around London in the early hours of the morning, to ponder his evolutionary theories. Dickens wrote his novels between the hours of 9 am and 2 pm and after that, he would go out for a long walk to regain inspiration. Woody Allen credits taking showers for helping him "unblock ideas". Salvador Dali was well known for sleeping with a key in hand so that he could come up with creative images during a half wake dream (alpha-theta) state known as hypnagogia.

> It sounds counterintuitive that focusing on just one task can actually hinder your ability for a creative solution.

But a compelling body of evidence shows that taking regular breaks from mental tasks greatly improves creative power. David Burkus, author of *The Myths of Creativity*, explains exactly why breaks, or periods of incubation, lead to creative breakthroughs: "One possible explanation for these findings is that when you work on a problem continuously, you can become fixated on a previous solution. Taking a break from the problem and focusing on something else entirely gives the mind some time to release its fixation on the same solutions and let the old pathways fade from memory. Then, when you return to the original problem, your mind is more open to new possibilities."[25]

In the ever-wise, Emma Seppälä's *The Happiness Track*, a whole chapter is dedicated to the science of "getting more done by doing nothing". The idea is that we need a healthy balance of both focus and rest. It is a case in point. If our minds are constantly processing information, we never give ourselves a chance to let our imagination take over and allow our thoughts to drift.

She says poignantly, "If we don't give our minds a break, they cannot engage in the kind of idle activity that leads to creative inspiration… When the mind is partially engaged, its resources are not overly taxed. It is free enough to forge unexpected, intriguing connections and to allow original ideas to bubble up to the surface."[26]

Similarly, if one were curious to know how and when our brains operate at peak level, several studies have been dedicated to the science of creativity and its relation to the frequency of our brainwaves. (Brainwaves are synchronised electrical impulses that enable different regions of the brain to communicate with each other.)

At any given moment, our brains emit different types of electrical patterns depending on the type of conscious state we experience. Examples of conscious states would be playing an instrument, exercising, sitting an exam, and so on. When we are awake and focused on performing cognitive tasks and problem solving, our brain emits beta waves (as talked about earlier) - characterised by active thinking and attentive focus. Although being in beta mode serves us well in daily tasks, the downside of excess beta activity is it can lead to feelings of stress and anxiety.

Alpha waves, by contrast, are emitted during intense and mindful states of relaxation; somewhat like a state of relaxed alertness. You would be most likely going into Alpha mode while relaxing into a long massage or perhaps even during a deep meditation.

> Understanding these patterns can really help you find a way towards achieving your 'AHA moments'.

Dr Joos Meyer, an expert on the science behind peak performance, writes about the importance of going into an Alpha state for peak creativity:

> "When faced with complex problems, creative people demonstrate bursts of alpha wave activity during moments of inspiration and insight. Less creative people do not show these big bursts of alpha. Similarly, the difference between elite and novice athletes can be seen in their brain activity. In the beginning, a novice athlete's brain shows very little alpha brain wave activity. The more experience, the more alpha. Just before their best free throws, an elite basket baller will produce a huge burst of alpha brain waves. Just before their best drives and just before their best shots, golfers, marksmen, and archers alike will show bursts of alpha brain wave activity."[27]

This data has huge implications for us. It could even possibly explain why sometimes we wake up in the middle of the night or early morning with a sudden breakthrough or a solution to a problem.

THE SECRETS TO PEAK INSPIRATION

So now we are aware that our brains work at its creative peak while under more relaxed conditions, let's look at some other practical ways to get our juices flowing.

Understand your Circadian Rhythm

If you've ever noticed that you tend to feel full of energy and/or lethargic around the same times every day, this is a perfect example of your circadian rhythm at work. This bodily rhythm is basically a 24-hour biological clock that operates in the background and regularly oscillates between drowsiness and alertness. Your circadian rhythm also can give you an accurate reading on whether you are a morning-type person or an evening-type person.

Your Best Time to Make Rational Decisions

Treating timing when making a strategic or important decision is the smartest thing you can do. This is largely because knowing what times of the day your biorhythms are most active, can actually help you become more productive and inch you closer towards breakthrough.

Studies have shown that the prefrontal cortex of the brain is most active when you wake up. What this means is that the mental energy required to perform activities is highest immediately after sleep. (However, night owls might have different peak times.) This is largely because the brain hasn't had to use any of its resources yet - important, rational and analytical decisions are best made at this time.

So if your task requires strong focus and careful concentration — such as editing your report, crunching some numbers, balancing spreadsheets or analysing literature — you are better off scheduling these tasks for your 'peak' time of the day. For most people that special time is in the morning. Also, because willpower generally fades towards the end of the day - morning is usually the best time to sit down and tackle things you have been procrastinating.

But what this also means is one should avoid looking at social media when you wake up.

You want to keep your brain energy high so you can tackle and make the best decisions. If this means putting your phone on airplane mode until you are done with your most important work, then so be it.

Your 'Aha!' Breakthroughs

While morning is considered an optimal time for cognitive performance, thought-provoking research suggests that not all problems can be solved during this time. This is because all problems are not the same and in fact some problems require us to think in an adhoc manner rather than systematically. In a study conducted by Mareike Wieth and Rose Zacks, participants were able to solve insight problems – problems that require more creativity rather than systematically working through it – during their non-optimal time of day (between 4:30 pm and 5:50 pm) as opposed to those who were given the task in the morning (between 8:30 am and 9:30 am).[28]

> Surprisingly, creativity jumps during off-peak times, when our mind loses focus and distracts easily.

It is in this state that you are much more likely to come up with novel ideas and 'Aha!' moments. Often referred to as the 'inspiration paradox', Psychologist Cindi May explains the reason for this increase in creativity: "At off-peak times we are less focused, and may consider a broader range of information. This wider scope gives us access to more alternatives and diverse interpretations, thus fostering innovation and insight."[29]

> So what this all tells us is that tasks that require our full concentration are better performed as soon as we wake up from sleep - whereas those that require us to think outside the box are better performed when our minds are more prone to distractions.

Take a Series of Mini Breaks

Are you aware that our brain can only hold forty-five minutes of purely focused attention, before its capacity to absorb information starts to decrease?

The give-away here is that if we are only engaged on one focused task, in order to maximise productivity we must take a series of mini breaks. For students, therefore, it would be a wise practice to study diligently for up to an hour and then take a small well-thought out break. If you are working on a project at work, you could leave your work area to go outside, listen to music, or go walk to a café to buy a coffee. The idea is to not heavily engage your brain with any newer information. If you'd like to kill two birds with one stone, combining movement with a relaxing activity such as forest bathing or brisk walking can stimulate the creativity areas in your brain.

> This is because when the body gets moving, the brain produces dopamine - the hormone associated with the brain's pleasure and reward system.

Even better, feeling relaxed while engaging in a task can also further trigger more dopamine flow.

Go into Alpha Mode

When under stress, our thinking becomes distorted because of our brain's instinct to divert energy to primitive regions responsible for fight or flight. As we know, our prefrontal cortex hence shuts down, and there is no room for creative or rational thinking. So, at this point it would be wise to move towards reaching an 'Alpha' state of mind. Anything that relaxes your body and releases tension can help one reach the Alpha state of mind, such as a relaxing walk, yoga, a guided meditation or even something as simple as just taking just five deep breaths.

Open Yourself to Distractions (And Away from Technology)

Find an activity - any activity - that takes you away from the solution you are trying to find. If you are stuck while writing a dissertation on 'frogs and their offspring', go ahead and read a totally different topic, perhaps even on space travel. If you are filing your documents and are feeling fatigued, take a leisurely dip into the pool. What this does is induce a phenomenon known as 'incubation'.

Adding onto Burkus's observations on incubation, Mark Fenske, cognitive-neuroscientist and co-author of *The Winner's Brain* explains that when we focus on a problem for an extended period of time, we tend to lean towards specific brain signals and suppress thoughts that our brain perceives to be unrelated to the task at hand. Taking a break and performing a different, less intellectually yet stimulating activity allows other parts of the brain to contribute. In a conversation with *The Boston Globe*, he humorously adds, "I sit in front of thousands of dollars worth of equipment and spend an embarrassing amount of time staring at the screen, then I get my best idea in the shower."[30]

Call of the Wild

It is no wonder that nature is described as our brain's miracle medicine, as well as a huge proponent in reducing attention fatigue. And now we have the science to back it up. Cognitive psychologists Ruth Ann Atchley, David Strayer and Paul Atchley believe that spending time in nature restores the depleted resources of our prefrontal cortex, which in turn helps us be more creative in problem-solving.

They explain that in our technological savvy society, we spend hours on our phones and computers thereby heavily utilizing "higher order cognitive functions"[31] such as focus, problem solving, inhibition and multi-tasking.

> So, if we think we are taking a break by checking our social media feeds, we are highly mistaken.

Sustained exposure to a natural setting, such as a walk in the park or a brief brush with nature, after a long period of focus gives a chance for our prefrontal cortex to physically recover. And this in turn inspires bursts of creativity when solving problems, as well as inducing a feeling of well-being. Have you ever wondered why you feel mentally and physically energised after going for a walk in the park? In fact, Seppälä believes even looking at photographs of nature for as little as 40 seconds can rejuvenate and boost your attention levels.[32]

Find Your Own Flow

Everyone has their own way of reaching an altered state of 'flow', and it is our responsibility to find it for ourselves. Be it to explore activities such as: chess, rock climbing, the arts, dance, listening to jazz, playing rummy, forest bathing, dancing, swimming, soul cycling, running, solving crosswords, stamping envelopes, washing the dishes, journaling — the possibilities are endless.

> Start looking for those unsuspecting pathways that can lead you to that state of flow.

Begin paying attention to that which makes you feel so immersed in what you are doing that there is little distinction between self and environment; and the past, present and future.

SUMMARY

Keeping the creative fire alive within us is paramount to our well-being and decision-making abilities. In addition, science proves that being in a state of creation helps decrease stress levels, increase brain health and longevity. When you are in state of creation or flow (away from survival mode), you are at the point of breakthrough and innovation.

Secrets to Peak Creativity

- **Understand Your Circadian Rhythm.** If you've ever noticed that you tend to feel full of energy and drowsy around the same times every day, this is a perfect example of your circadian rhythm at work. Keep track and note down your cycles of energy and lethargy levels, that is, your peak and off-peak timings.

- **Your Best Time to Make Rational Decisions.** Studies have shown that the prefrontal cortex of the brain is most active when you wake up. Because the brain hasn't had to use its resources yet, rational and analytical decisions (such as number crunching, mathematical tasks or reading a report) are best made at this time.

- **Your 'Aha!' Breakthrough.** Also known as the inspiration paradox, there is an upside to that afternoon slump you feel after lunch. Inspirational breakthroughs are found to be more prevalent during your afternoons.

- **Take Mini Breaks.** Because our brain can only focus for 45 minutes at a stretch, we need to take frequent breaks to allow our brain to *recover*. Even better, combining a break with movement (forest walking or stretching) is great for further breakthroughs, due to the burst of endorphins.

- **Go into Alpha Mode.** When under stress, our thinking becomes distorted because of our brain's instinct to divert energy to primitive regions responsible for fight or flight. Hence, our prefrontal cortex shuts down, and there is no room for creative or rational thinking. So, at this point it would be wise to move towards the 'Alpha' state of mind. Anything that relaxes your body and releases tension can help you reach the Alpha state of mind. This can be anything from yoga and meditation to even just taking five deep breaths.

- **Open Yourself to Distractions (which do not involve technology).** The more of a contrast there is in the distraction, you are instigating something special called an incubation period. This period is good for problem solving and creative thinking.

- **Call of the Wild.** Spending time in nature or with nature restores depleted resources of the brain, which in turn helps us to be more open to creativity and problem-solving

- **Find Your Own Version of Flow.** Start looking for ways to arrive at that unique state of expression called flow, in which you are so immersed in your task that you lose sense of space and time.

Chapter 3

Integrity
Connecting To Your Truth

"To thine own self be true, and it must follow, as the night the day, thou canst not then be false to any man."

Hamlet, William Shakespeare

Can you recall the last time in your life you said "yes" when you should have really said "no"? Or when you had promised to commit to something, and then for some reason could not deliver? Some of us might have even said "yes" to big commitments like marriage, a new job, or moving countries—decisions made in haste masked behind fear and obligation. It is no wonder we experience guilt when we do not honour our word when in actuality, our hearts were never in it in the first place. The problem is, if we continue to engage in such behaviour regularly, there is a high chance we'll live out of alignment with who it is we really stand for. This phenomenon of inauthenticity starts leaking into every corner of our lives, as we silently allow outside expectations to come in the way of our core values. As a result, we slowly begin to lose a sense of integrity - visibly to others - but eventually towards our own selves. This Chapter reveals how vital it is for our own well-being to live in accordance with integral actions. It also uncovers how our body and brain react when we are not in alignment with our core values, as well as some practical life tools to bring us back into the driver's seat again.

Let's call it as it is - a person who exudes integrity holds a certain silent language about themselves. This indisputable language is often associated with someone who is boldly honest; who upholds strong moral principles and is highly ethical in nature and temperament.

(If we were to just pause for a moment, we certainly can think of someone in our lives who exudes this quality.)

But there is actually a whole other layer to integrity that often gets glossed over and is rarely talked about. If you open up any dictionary, you'll know that the word integrity evolved from the Latin word *integritas*, meaning whole or complete. Predictably, it is also related to the word integrate, which means "bringing together". In this sense, if one were to look at it from an abstract angle - being in integrity with oneself is akin to an integration of our outer life and our inner life. It is almost like two sides of a battle merging together creating a union. Being in integrity, therefore, is not just for other people – in fact, the virtue helps to make *you* feel better and more complete.

The type of integrity we are referring to can only really occur when the actions that one makes enables a sensation of congruency within. Real integrity is when our inner feelings match our outer actions or when our 'gut' tells us that we are doing the right thing. In contrast to society's externally imposed morality and ethics, a person of real integrity responds to and is guided by

'What does this action really mean to me?'

Staying committed to our internal state of being means we do not stray away from our own convictions; we listen closely to our gut reactions; and we respond appropriately by paying attention to that little voice in our heads which ultimately guides us towards the right thing to do. This is why being in integrity with ourselves, first and foremost, is absolutely key to building an unwavering and strong self-identity. In this light, no one can come in your way or make you do something you do not want to do.

It's easy to appear like a person of moral character when people are watching, but the true test of integrity lies in this:

> **Do you live your private life with the same level of consistency as you live your public life?**

Unfortunately, so much of our lives are consumed with "image maintenance". We spend vast amounts of energy trying to have people to think about us the way we want to be thought about. As a result, we slap on artificial social masks and the "perfect persona" around people to seek validation. John Ortberg, an evangelical Christian author, puts it so eloquently, "Human conversation is largely an endless attempt to convince others that we are more assertive or clever or gentle or successful than they might think if we did not carefully educate them."

Recently I was asked to give an impromptu speech at a friend's milestone birthday dinner and quite unlike myself - I froze. Put on the spot, everyone staring at me - a sudden thought flashed in my mind "What would be the smartest and sassiest thing to say?" The urge to suddenly please everyone was overwhelming. But in the process, I forgot about my friend. I forgot about the qualities that really drew me towards her. I forgot about the time she offered to go back to her house during a social gathering, just to pick up a shawl for me. I forgot that when I was new in town needed to get my bearings, she was one of the first people to extend a hand and take me for workshops that she knew I found interesting. I forgot that what I loved most about her was her ability to listen intently to whatever gripes I had - with no quick judgement. In that split second while put on the spot, I forgot about all these qualities and things I loved about her. And although I ticked all the boxes in the speech entertainment department, I completely blanked out on all those wonderful assets she had.

And this is the sad thing – we all do this in a myriad of ways, innocently and unknowingly. But this is where the problem really unravels in our lives. When we dismiss these little lapses of people-pleasing as 'no big deal' - eventually, they add up to form a giant snowball of inauthenticity. With this new awareness, I started catching these slips of character in many different places.

Seeing a message pop up on my screen and purposefully ignoring it for later.

Pretending to be busy on my phone and ignoring the chatty security guard on my way out for a walk.

Complaining to my kids about having to attend an event and then dragging them for it, too!

The Dreaded "I Have To" List

During a recent bout of overwhelm, I had called a friend to ask her advice on how she manages to balance her busy schedule. She agreed to meet me at the local Starbucks, and as we sat down in the midst of all the shuffling chairs and crying babies, she listened intently as I divulged about juggling my business, the house, the kids, the social events and... (you get the picture.) It was pure catharsis! And somewhere in between all the rambling, she just raised her hand, leaned forward and said "No wonder you are feeling overwhelmed. You are completely operating out of a have-to mentality".

Boy, she was right! She then asked me to write down two lists covering my daily activities over a span of seven days. The first list would be comprised of the tasks that I felt obliged or compelled to do – and the clue would be in my internal talk such as "I have to", "I should" and "I need to". And the second list of things was to be those activities that I found joy out of, wanted to do or resonated with - leading with internal talk saying, "I want to" or "I love to". Against each list, I was to write the advantages and disadvantages next to each activity, primarily directed towards my own well-being. This would help me weave out which activities I could keep and which I could eventually eliminate.

> **Quite simply, was I motivated to do things out of 'love' or out of 'fear'?** ➤

List 1 was full of events - obligations, openings, baby showers, birthdays, extended familial duties - not really things I wanted to do but ones that fulfilled my "have to" list. To my astonishment, List 2 was almost empty. No wonder I was in a state of overwhelm.

The bottom line was this. With all the things that I felt compelled to do, I had simply lost contact with the activities that gave me real joy in life. I had forgotten what it felt like to have my fingers cathartically glide across the piano keys, as I would lose myself to Beethoven's Moonlight Sonata. I had forgotten how I would fall into a relaxed and flowing state behind a pottery wheel and come out feeling alive again. I forgot what it felt like to take my dogs to the beach and playfully dunk into the water with them. And, of course, there was so much more.

All it took was a snap list like this for me to appreciate that I was living a life which did not resonate with my whole sense of well-being. So, what was it that had gotten me trapped in this spiral? As I traced it down, I realised that firstly - I had forgotten what it felt like to say no to others when it did not suit my schedule. If I were to look even deeper, the fear of upsetting others was too great a burden to bear. Second - the fear of missing out on something that could have been of value to me with regards to work or society, was also driving me to attend as many events event possible. As a result of these two misleading factors, I forgot what it really meant to be true to myself and my needs. I was living life not for myself, but rather for others.

With just this simple revelation, my life started naturally streamlining into activities or projects that were good for my own mental well-being.

My new principle became this - if the activity does not bring me internal peace, laughter, inspired action, monetary gain, or increased physical energy - I can and easily will say no.

The Price We Pay When We Live Out of Integrity

When convenient, the brain is extremely apt at justifying our white lies and our pretences. After all, if we are not harming another human being, we justify by thinking it can't be all that bad. But studies show that we are affected adversely when we act of out of alignment with what we truly mean.

Even A Little Dishonesty Causes Stress to Our Bodies

Let's call a spade a spade. Pretending to be or feel something that you don't - even if it is a small thing or is designed to protect someone else's feelings - is still considered to be a form of dishonesty. In fact, research points out that even the smallest lies actually create physical stress to our brains and bodies. Have you ever wondered how polygraph tests (also known as lie detectors) work? Polygraphs don't actually detect the lie itself. They detect lies through measuring changes in our skin electricity, pulse rate and breathing. In other words, they detect the subconscious stress and fear that lying is caused by.

Keeps Us In A State of Anxiety

Don't all of us want to believe that at heart, we are good and moral human beings? Of course, the majority of humans strive to feel this way. But when we indulge in a choice or make a decision that doesn't feel quite right, a gap opens up between our actual behaviour and our self-image. A certain type of mental anxiety takes over, also known as cognitive dissonance. In the field of psychology, cognitive dissonance is the mental discomfort which is experienced by a person who simultaneously holds two or more contradictory beliefs, ideals or values. In *A Theory of Cognitive Dissonance* (1957), Leon Festinger proposed that "human beings strive for internal psychological consistency in order to mentally function in the real world."[33]

A person who experiences internal inconsistencies tends to become psychologically uncomfortable. Of course, since no one likes this feeling of discomfort, our brains quickly attempt to bridge the gap between our "negative" actions and our positive self-image. This is when we justify to ourselves that our behaviour was 'really not so bad, after all.' The danger is, the more we do this - the more we are at risk of living out of alignment with ourselves and it develops into an incessant cycle.

In fact, some doctors have also attributed one of the biggest hidden causes of anxiety and depression connected to a person living out of sync with his or her values. Dr. Alan Weiss, the Medical Director of Annapolis Integrative Medicine, advises people with chronic depression to "clean up any integrity issues you may have in your life"[34]. This has huge implications for those of us who do not have access to a clear value system and hence suffer as a result.

The Domino Effect

This leads to a poignant quote by Piero Ferucci, from his book, *The Power of Kindness*: "Lying has a thousand faces. The truth only one."[35]

Indeed, like a chain of dominoes falling one by one, one lie or falsehood will never be enough. Committing a dishonest act in one area of your life often bleeds into other areas. Why? Just like the expression "if you tell the truth, you do not have to remember anything", if you are dishonest in your life at some point you will eventually have to back up your previous lies or social personas in the future. Recently, I watched an episode of *Revenge Body*, where one of the contestants who had a huge following on Instagram, and also happens to be severely overweight. As the season progressed, he found himself crumbling under the pressure not of the show, but rather of his own lies. This was because some time back, he had created a false body image online to impress and gain more followers on Instagram. The truth was, the disparity between his real-life overweight body and the 'fit body' he represented on social media, (via filters), was too huge to even provide a fair comparison. If he was at a mall for example - upon being spotted and hearing a fan call out his name he would immediately scramble and hide behind a corner so as not to expose his real body size. Of course, he constantly lived under stress and anxiety as he felt he could never meet his followers face to face, for fear of embarrassment. This type of deception is a very slippery slope, as the research shows that small lies make it easier to tell bigger lies.

An article written by Brett & Kate McKay, also authors of *The Art of Manliness*, divulge the chain-effect that just one simple lie can cause.

"Once you commit one dishonest act, your moral standards loosen, your self-perception as an honest person gets a little hazier, your ability to rationalise goes up, and your fudge factor margin increases."[36]

Harder to Focus

It's a mystery to a lot of us why we find it so much easier to stick to our diets early in the morning, but as the day wears on we find ourselves progressively losing our self-discipline.

By nightfall, we might even find ourselves seeking out the hidden dark chocolate from the depths of our fridge. This phenomenon can be explained through understanding how our minds handle self-control. Just like a muscle, the act of self-control in reality has a short lifespan of sorts as the ability to repeatedly exert willpower is quite limited. It is similar to the functioning of a muscle that is constantly moving - once it tires and can no longer perform at peak strength, the muscle eventually just gives in. On the same trajectory, the very act in itself is also a brain drain and erodes the power to focus and do other deep work.

Now, we may not realise it but when we pretend - a certain amount of self-control is exhausted, and it hence weakens our will-power muscle later on. To cite an example, research shows that the little fib you told your friend at the supermarket about how well you are doing even though you could be in the midst of a crisis, will genuinely create a subconscious reaction and make it harder for you to focus later on. What this means is a fake performance or an attempt to hide who you really are or how you are really feeling has a profound effect on your behaviour. It depletes the energy that is needed to control your emotions; your ability to engage deeply and efficiently in a task; and it might even cause you to react more aggressively to a provocation. On the contrary, when we are honest about how we feel or what we mean, a whole burden is lightened, and we feel in tune with ourselves.

People can Smell Insincerity

Warren Buffet, Chairman and CEO of Berkshire Hathaway, said it best:

"In looking for people to hire, look for three qualities: integrity, intelligence, and energy. And if they don't have the first one, the other two will kill you."

It is no secret that people of integrity are highly attractive for leadership positions. Moreover, if we are trying to make a good impression, our bodies and expressions do not lie.

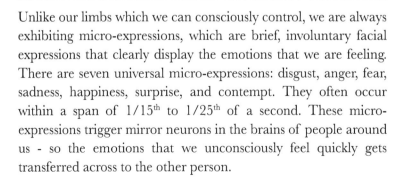

Insincerity and inauthenticity permeate not just from our words or actions, but also largely on a subconscious level.

Unlike our limbs which we can consciously control, we are always exhibiting micro-expressions, which are brief, involuntary facial expressions that clearly display the emotions that we are feeling. There are seven universal micro-expressions: disgust, anger, fear, sadness, happiness, surprise, and contempt. They often occur within a span of $1/15^{th}$ to $1/25^{th}$ of a second. These micro-expressions trigger mirror neurons in the brains of people around us - so the emotions that we unconsciously feel quickly gets transferred across to the other person.

You know when you get a good feeling about someone?

The chances are that your brain probably picked up on their positive micro-expressions or their authentic and congruent body language. On the contrary, people who are prone to fibbing or putting on a social persona to pretend they're something they're not, surprisingly also transmit negative emotions. And due to the phenomenon of cognitive dissonance, those negative feelings simply cannot be hidden. So, the bottom line is - humans are not very good at hiding how they feel.

Risk of Becoming A 'Drifter'

Every now and then, we wade into certain decisions because of outside pressures or because of a phenomenon known as social compliance. We might find ourselves taking the 'better safe than sorry' route or perhaps satisfying someone else's needs, in order to make our decision. This is also known as drifting. In the late 90s', I was accepted into one of the most prestigious business schools in the UK. Much like most 18-year olds, being thrown into a life-long decision is no easy task and the enthrallment of being associated with a prestigious name ended up becoming the basis of my future. Even though I had a slight inkling that Social Psychology would eventually be my lifelong passion, a concerned elder told me quite poignantly, "a psychology degree would take up too many years of your life." I ended up taking the path of least resistance: the conventional, mainstream and popular Business and Management degree. I eventually found it to be lacklustre and somewhat misaligned to my real interest - understanding what makes people tick. Of course, in retrospect, it seemed like a practical and strategic way to spend a few years and I figured it would keep my options open later. However, being young and impressionable, I did not really delve too much on the long-term consequences of my decision. As it turns out, going to Business School was a fortunate twist of fate for my career, because I discovered many facets of people management, one such being NLP. So, sometimes if you are lucky, this phenomenon of 'drift' can lead you to your path, but that doesn't always hold true. Who knows? If I had followed what my soul was calling towards me at the time, I would have run away with a degree in Social Psychology. And just perhaps, my career would have propelled me onto a completely different path. So, the risk of not being aligned to your own values, is that you do not live a life of real intention.

> And when you are not living in intention, outward circumstances also known as 'life' will drag you to places which may or may not be suitable for you or be aligned to your soul's calling.

How valuable is this for our children to know as they are to make big decisions in life?

THE TRICKS OUR BRAINS PLAY ON US

Although the pressures to conform creates an ideal social persona for the outside world, our evolutionary brain also has a lot to contribute towards how we resist living a life of integrity.

What lies at the root of our decisions to compromise on our very own principles?

What factors lead us to be dishonest and what behaviours can help us be more upright?

And how do our decision-making skills get affected by stressful situations?

So, let's look at some internal obstacles which block us from living a principle-driven life.

The Common Mental Short-Cut

Do you find yourself coming up with white lies when put on the spot or while answering an uncomfortable question? Left to its own devices when faced with a sudden and challenging situation, your brain will take shortcuts wherever it can. In the field of psychology, these mental shortcuts are known as heuristics, and they act as a way for the brain to conserve energy and work more efficiently. Indeed, these little tricks and "rules of thumb" allow us to quickly make judgments and solve problems effectively. The issue arises when our brain's inclination towards efficiency short-circuits our own integrity.

This explains why, at times when we're caught between a rock and a hard place, we will instinctively go with the easier option. For example, turning down your neighbour's kind offer of help at your daughter's birthday party seems like the easiest thing to do in the moment, although in actuality you would not mind the helping hand. The white lie covers up a solution where short-term gain is more attractive; sparing your neighbour the effort of blowing up balloons or avoiding feeling obligated to her in the future. But this leaves you feeling short-changed because realistically there is no way all those balloons can be blown up in an hour - and you are left stressed and out of time.

In Fear of Loss

Because of our innate need to belong and feel accepted, we might lean on the belief that conforming to society is one of the keystones to self-fulfilment. But, when this tendency becomes an overarching goal, it turns us into 'people pleasers'. People pleasing is a process of trying to determine what other people want, or what will make them think favourably of us, and hence acting accordingly. At times, we think we cannot say no. We feel compelled to do things that we do not want to do, due to the fear of someone else becoming upset and hence ostracising us from a group. We might even find ourselves acting just like the people around us.

People pleasers constantly need external praise to feel good about themselves. They tend not to admit when their feelings are hurt and in this way, they lose a sense of their precious boundaries. People that live in this state are also living in fear of loss of reputation, fear of rejection or criticism. This tendency can also be traced back to our childhood, where we were taught that 'other's opinions really matter', (perhaps even more than our own). We were probably also taught to believe that what others thought of us was paramount and we could not bear being embarrassed in public.

> At some point, other's opinions started to matter more than our own. ✈

We experience this in small, tight communities - where our reputation is highly reliant on how we present ourselves to the rest of the society. We portray ourselves to be virgins until marriage; throw lavish parties to show our financial success; show off our charitable armour to gain honour; and the like – all in vain to gain approval from the community.

> And sometimes we even fool ourselves into believing that pleasing others is the same as helping others. ✈

But any time we pretend to be something we are not, the true acid test lies in whether our actions are dependent on what others think about us. The answer will tell us immediately if we are acting out of integrity with ourselves or just acting in a way to please the world around us.

Inability to Know or Trust One's Intuition

Sometimes, our inner voice has been muffled for so long, we have forgotten what it is like to listen to our very sacred intuition. There has been a plethora of research to prove that the more we pay attention to our intuition, the better our decision making becomes and progressively develops over time.

A study on gambling was recently conducted by Neuroscientist Antonio Damasio, in which stress markers were measured during the decision-making process. He concluded by saying that when making tough decisions, it is important to pay attention to "somatic markers"[37]. Somatic markers are feelings in the body that are associated with different emotions, such as the association of rapid heartbeat with anxiety or of nausea with disgust. Originating in the insula - the part of the brain that is responsible for social emotions like pride or guilt - and merging with the amygdala (which cues our response to threats) - the somatic markers relay messages that alert us if something feels off.

Of course then, if we find ourselves struggling to make a decision, it would make sense to tap into our bodies' emotional responses. In this way, we can also be sure that we are remaining in integrity to ourselves. This also explains why the term 'gut reaction' has become so mainstream in conversations surrounding decision making.

Your Role Models Have Turned Out Fine

It is quite possible that we have witnessed those around us who are parents, relatives, bosses, or even friends - who may have not necessarily lived a life of real integrity. In fact, not only have they not gotten away with it, but perhaps even turned out to be successful at what they do. But what we might forget is everyone has their own measuring stick for life satisfaction, and because people are experts at covering their emotions - we really have no idea what their internal makeup feels like. They could be feeling jaded, shameful, guilty, etc. and possibly just not aware of it. On the other hand, they could even have fooled themselves into believing like they are living their life with integrity, and are quite happy to continue that way.

Getting Back into the Driver's Seat

Almost every single day we are faced with little decisions that reflect the integrity of our life. I love Charles Marshall's famous quote from his book *Shattering the Glass Slipper*, defining integrity as "doing the right thing when you don't have to—when no one else is looking or will ever know—when there will be no congratulations or recognition for having done so."[38]

Let's face it. There is a robust sense of personal satisfaction that comes from being truthful. It feels good to 'keep it real' - not just to others - but also to ourselves. Here are some ways to regain control over your own integrity, especially if you feel you are drifting.

How to Revisit your Value System

There is a valuable visualisation technique I used to practice during the throes of anxiety:

> Close your eyes, and in your mind's eye, imagine an older you reflecting back on everything you stand for in your current life. Picture yourself as if on a movie screen, watching your current self move around. What values and characteristics define you as a human being? What do you look like? What are you doing with your time? Where are you? Who is in your life? With this image in your mind, think about how you want to be remembered. Keep this vision and feeling close to you as you write out a new value list.

What is important to note is that values are not just related to your likes and dislikes. Instead, values represent what is important to you.

Now you are ready with the process of realigning your actions to what really matters to you. Similar to the "have to" list, go ahead and plot down the things you do every day which rob you of your inner peace (keeping in mind your older-self looking back at you.) Then start crossing out the things that do not align with your 'value system' and start including a new 'action list'.

If you are feeling stuck on crafting out a values/action list, here is an example below:

Value:

I value spending more time with people I love, knowing that someday they will not be in my lives anymore.

Action:

Visit my grandmother in India every few months.

Practice more eye contact when my children are talking to me.

Say no to unnecessary events that do not include the people on my list.

Practice Small

With the idea of progress and not perfection in mind - start honouring those small commitments and promises you have made to yourself with the intent of enhancing your own well-being. Each small step you take towards honouring your commitments and your word will in fact help you gain more confidence to be yourself with others in a more authentic manner. Here are a few valuable tips to getting started:

- Avoid telling small white lies, no matter how insignificant or trivial they may be.
- Practice showing up on time. Being on time not only shows virtue of character but it also teaches you that you can depend on yourself. This is because the more promises you can stick to, the more your self-confidence increases. In the bargain, you will also feel more in control of your life and less subject to the mercy of bad habits and compulsions.
- Be impeccable with your word. As Toltec Author, Don Miguel Ruiz very aptly states in 'The Four Agreements', "Speak with integrity. Say only what you mean. Avoid using the Word to speak against yourself or to gossip about others. Use the power of your Word in the direction of truth and love."[39]

Mix up your Circle

Jim Rohn, a well-known American motivation expert, could not have been more accurate when he said, "You are the average of the five people you spend the most time with."

> To back his theory up - there is some very credible evidence to support that when two people are in the company of each other, their brain waves begin to appear nearly identical. ➤

In fact, thanks to people such as well-known neuroscientist Moran Cerf, from Northwestern University, we now have clues as to how decisions are made. He concluded after studying a group of moviegoers, that the most engaging trailers all produced similar patterns in people's brains.

"The more we study engagement, we see time and again that just being next to certain people actually aligns your brain with them."[40]

In line with this, it would then make sense to, make an effort to engage with people who stand true to themselves and their value systems. Some examples of this would be to be in the presence of people who have found a cause they believe in; who are not shy of exposing their vulnerabilities; and people who have been loyal to you while you were at your lowest.

Apologising when Necessary

Apology is not just a social nicety, it is a sign of courage and humility. Saying "I am sorry" or "I was wrong" is an important ritual - a way of showing respect for a relationship that could have disintegrated due to misunderstanding. Apologies also incite the other person to trust you and feel safe around you. But most importantly, there is an unquestionable sense of freedom you experience when you apologise. I like to think of it as a healing process because metaphorically speaking when "we keep our side of the street clean"[41], we unconsciously release a heavy burden on our hearts.

Being Vulnerable

As Hannah Brencher, a motivational speaker and author, says **"It's okay to be not okay."** We live in a culture that is rife with opinions and judgement - and it has become exceptionally easy to fool the world into thinking we are happy, popular, or successful. In fact, showing our vulnerabilities openly is almost non-existent in our social media savvy world. Growing up with the idea that vulnerability is a weakness hits the people-pleasing nerve in our heads and is possibly our biggest downfall, because sometimes we do wake up tired and broken. Instead of living from a highlight reel of successes, a core component to maintaining our integrity is to keep it real with others and speak the truth. Although we might be trying to feel better by putting on a happy face for others, we know that pretending always backfires in the end. And also, your close relationships and friendships will benefit too, as being vulnerable enables people to trust you a whole lot more as you express yourself more authentically.

Say No

A healthy sense of self requires creating firm boundaries.

In this light, it also means having the ability to say no to things you do not have time or value for. "We live under this misconception that saying yes, being available, always at the ready for other people, makes us a better person, but in fact it does quite the opposite. You get stressed and anxious; you're viewed as a patsy," according to Susan Newman, social psychologist and author of *The Book of No*.[42] In fact, setting boundaries around your life reasserts your own self-respect and as a result, others will also respect you more.

SUMMARY

Being in integrity with oneself involves not just being true to your commitments, but more importantly reflects a congruency between your inner feelings and your outer actions. Living in integrity means you are true to your own principles and values and do not need to pretend to be someone you are not.

Alas, there is a heavy price to pay when we are not congruent with our values, principles and truths.

- **Dishonesty Causes Stress to Our Bodies.** Lying, even a small white lie meant to protect someone else, actually creates physical stress to our brains and bodies.
- **Prone to Anxiety.** A certain anxiety, also known as cognitive dissonance, takes over when our inner feelings don't match our outer actions.
- **The Domino Effect.** Being insincere in one area of your life often bleeds into other areas. (This is because eventually, you will have to back up your previous white lies, social personas, and acts.)
- **Harder to Focus.** A performance or an attempt to hide who you really are diverts energy that is needed to control your emotions. It also effects your ability to engage deeply and efficiently in a task. In fact, at times it might even cause you to react more aggressively to a provocation.
- **People Can Smell Insincerity.** Simply put, our bodies do not lie. Subconsciously we are adept at picking up cues through micro-facial expressions and inconspicuous body language. Not only this, people who pretend to be someone they are not unconsciously transmit negative emotions, (because of the phenomenon of cognitive dissonance).

So, how do we get ourselves back into the driver's seat? We can practice the below actions:

- Re-examine our values and principles again. (Visualisation Exercise/Value and action list on page 142-3).
- Practice with small actions. Avoid white lies, reach places on time, and always speak your truth.
- Mix with people who say what they mean and mean what they say!
- Don't be afraid to apologise when you are at fault
- Allow yourself to feel vulnerable in front of others.
- Learn to say no, when you really want to!

CHAPTER 4

HUMILITY
AN UNEXPLORED POWER

"Do you wish to rise? Begin by descending."
Saint Augustine of Hippo (5ᵗʰ Century)

In today's social media-obsessed society, the true essence of humility appears to be slowly dissipating. The famous poet Alfred Lord Tennyson wrote in The Holy Grail, that humility is "the highest virtue, the mother of them all"[43]. But in a world that celebrates over-confidence, narcissism and self-entitlement - how does one really remain humble? And what do we stand to gain from keeping this virtue steadfast in our lives?

A wise man once said...

"Go through your day with a note in your left pocket that says 'for my sake the world was created.' Put another note with the words 'I am but dust and ashes' in your right pocket."

This man was none other than Rabbi Simcha Bunim of Peshicha (1765-1827), who was known for preaching this method with a profound truth in mind: that each individual being *is* important to this world, but not enough to actually feel self-important. (A paradox of sorts, but a great reminder by a brilliant visionary.)

The verity is - we all are born into this world with nothing but our innocence and childlike wonder. Then, as a natural part of growing up, our innocence is slowly stripped away by society's conditioning. Through absorbing opinions and ideas from people close to us and from our environment, it is gradually ingrained in us that in order to exist or amount to 'something' in life, we need to prove ourselves to the world. The setback is, if we continue to take this entitled attitude to the grave, we are really only damaging one person - and that is of course, ourselves.

When we forget the essence of humility, we are limiting what provides us with true wholesome human potential.

We lose out on the ability to laugh at ourselves because we are too consumed with looking silly.

We neglect to love others with reckless abandon because we are afraid to be vulnerable.

We forget what it is like to give sincerely and without expectation because we live in a state of giving equals reward.

We lose our serenity because we have the pressure to prove our accomplishments on a day to day basis.

And it goes on…

In the same light, being on constant 'show' is possibly the largest source of human misery. This stems from our society's constant and exhausting need for external validation to' feel good' about ourselves. As we will explore later on, attachment to external validation has many flaws. First and foremost, the satisfaction is fleeting and highly addictive. Hence it is damaging to our self-esteem and morale if we do not receive outside approval. Lastly it can lead us astray from ourselves - by a phenomenon known as 'drifting' discussed earlier.

BECOMING MORE SELF-AWARE WITH HUMILITY

The concept of being humble is nothing new, but at times, its power and potency is underestimated and misunderstood. It must be noted that humility is not a facade to be put on for the outside world - in fact it is an internally cultivated virtue to be sought after.

Mother Teresa called humility the premise of all virtues. She held that, "If you are humble nothing will touch you, neither praise nor disgrace, because you know what you are. If you are blamed you will not be discouraged. If they call you a saint you will not put yourself on a pedestal."

This rings true on many levels because when we experience an enduring state of humility, we are very much aware of our own faults and shortcomings. In fact, we are able to identify our mistakes immediately as soon as they crop up - without the need to justify or reject them. And because of our strong sense of self-awareness, no one can come in the way of interfering or trying to measure our self-worth.

A renewed interest into the concept of humility has recently prompted psychologists to explore exactly how the very act affects our brains. Psychologist Pelin Kesebir, who found multi-fold benefits to humility, recently conducted one such famous study. In her study, Kesebir borrowed the term "a quiet ego"[44] from Wayment and Bauer and further explained her own perspective on it by saying that humility "involves a willingness to accept the self's limits and its place in the grand scheme of things."

She describes a humble person as someone with "a strong sense of self-mastery – they know what they're good at and what they're bad at, and they don't seek praise or confirmation from their peers because they neither want nor need it."

So, with enough practice a humble person can tap into a deep well of self-understanding and self-awareness, while also masterfully escaping the addiction of external validation. And we can finally grasp onto that feeling that we are 'enough' without the need for anyone telling us so.

A Distinction: Humility is Not Modesty

Some people equate humility with modesty. Likewise, modesty is also often considered synonymous with humility, but unlike true humility - it is often artificial and externally oriented. For example, modesty could be described as the reluctance to show off, put oneself on display or to attract attention. But here is the catch - stooping low for the sake of others is again another way of expecting some form of validation from the outside world.

True humility, on the other hand, is acquired from a clear perspective of the human condition: that we are one amongst billions of other people on a small planet, amongst a billion planets. Or in simpler terms, a realisation befalls that our beings carry no more value or importance than whoever we meet.

So here, a clear distinction is drawn. The act of humility itself is to subdue our ego so that things are no longer just about us. On the other hand, to be modest is to protect the ego of others so they do not feel threatened or uncomfortable.

How Pain Can Bring Us Back to Reality

Imagine it being a fairly standard morning and everything is routinely going well. You reach work in the nick of time, reply to your emails and head out to the nearest coffee shop for your usual morning cuppa. Then, while reaching for your mobile phone in your purse, you realise it's not in its usual spot. Next, you fumble your fingers around within all the other pockets of your bag as a desperate attempt to find it. Finally, you find an empty table and dump all the contents of your bag onto it, but - it's still missing.

Your world comes crashing down as you crumble into a chair and try to remember the last time you made a call.

Was it at the laundromat? It can't be because you remember leaving with your clothes all bundled in your arms and calling your husband to open the door for you.

It must be at the theatre that you went to the day before! That's where it must be. Rapidly, it seems like your world is being brought to a standstill as all you can think about is finding this electronic glass and metal gadget which has pretty much taken over your life (and not to mention your mental well-being.) Suddenly, you notice that the emotions you are feeling are ironically mixed. You are knee-deep in anxiety from the shock of leaving it behind somewhere. Yet you are also ironically a little excited from all the chaos and also dreading the thought of updating a new phone. You also notice a sense of vulnerability because your most precious device could be in someone else's hands. These emotions start showing itself, as you frantically call up the theatre from the barista's landline. You become fretful and lose hope as they ask you to wait until they locate the manager in charge.

Fifteen minutes later, still on hold, you're still standing knuckles clenched around the landline. You are envisaging all the numbers you need to retrieve; all the photos that you have lost; and all the apps you need to painfully download again. Suddenly the manager's voice comes back on the line and tells you that they have your phone in their possession, all locked up in a safe.

The world is back to order again and you are shrouded in relief.

Despite the anxious and vulnerable emotions you were experiencing just fifteen minutes ago, you are suddenly overwhelmed with a deep sense of gratitude. You are certainly thankful that you don't need to buy a new phone and deal with all the complexities that go with it. You feel indebted that people cared enough to keep it locked away in a safe. And perhaps you are even touched by the empathetic look from the barista.

It is no wonder that the feeling of gratitude lends itself to a profound sense of humility.

The simple awareness that people around you have the ability to empathise, help and share similar emotions with makes you feel a sense of unity. You walk out of the coffee shop feeling a strong sense of appreciation, hope and relief - very different from how you felt walking in.

Of course, there's nothing more humbling than a mere brush with a life and death experience. At times, it takes a traumatic life experience to help realign our sense of humility. If you can imagine…

You are two hours into a flight with violent turbulence when suddenly the crackled sound of the pilot's voice announces that there needs to be a diversion due to bad weather. You fearfully observe other passengers firmly gripping their armrests as the plane dips up and down with wild abandon, during its descent through the stormy clouds. In those moments, the only thought that runs through your mind is how you forgot to tell your kids you loved them before you dropped them to school this morning. As the unsteady plane approaches the runway, you are quivering feverishly, filled with dread.

At last, the plane lands with a thud - and the rest of the passengers are crying sighs of relief, joy and exchanging hugs all around as you sit there numb with relief. You look around at every passenger, all from different origins, ages and backgrounds, and it hits you - we are all equal on this journey of life. After you've had a chance to regain your composure, you start thinking a bit more clearly about what transpired. You are shot back into reality.

The truth is, humbling experiences such as this, revamps our understanding of the world. Sometimes we are so locked up in our own individualism, we overlook that we really are no more 'special than', 'greater than', or 'less than' others. In a sense, those invisible barriers that we all unconsciously keep with one another only can exist when there is no shared experience of crisis and pain. This is because in general, humans have a natural tendency to come together in support when they sense someone is in crisis. After all, we are all human - experiencing the same type of emotions, going through similar hardships, and facing the same fears. Hence, in times of crisis, the desire to prove greatness and 'put on a show' to one another is reduced significantly. It is a funny paradox - that this gift of humility sometimes greets us in our most painful moments, bringing us back to earth and helping us to feel more grounded.

Piero Ferrucci, in *The Power of Kindness*, puts it so beautifully:

"We realise our humanness: we are fallible and vulnerable."[45]

BEING HUMBLE: WHY DO WE CARE?

To no one's fault, the detrimental belief that we are different and 'special' from one other is a product of what we are taught as young children. Introduction to school and immersion into society stages the formation of ego and a false sense of 'entitlement'. (This being said, one way to introduce and balance humility into our children's lives, is to enunciate that they are not special, but the efforts that they make are.)

If you think about it, why does the virtue of humility hold so much weight amongst the greatest minds and propagated by so many world leaders? It is not only because it is an appeasing quality to have and of course, a pleasant experience to be around someone who is in check with themselves. There is so much else to it.

> The truth is: humility empowers us greatly.

Rabbi Jonathan Sacks says humility 'is one of the most expansive and life-enhancing of all virtues'[46]. Sometimes we unconsciously perceive humility to be a sign of weakness, but that is an unfortunate fallacy. A humble person does not, by any means, undervalue themselves but instead, possesses an openness to life's opportunities. What this means is that because they are humble enough to realise that they do not know everything, their door is always open to possibilities and new ideas.

Hence, practising humility places us in a capacity where a good amount of self-learning takes place and educating ourselves further becomes conceivable. Herein, lies a huge well of potential for insightful self-growth.

In *Alcoholics Anonymous*, a 'humble' chance is given to the recovering addict. As part of the spiritual program, one of their tasks is to take a moral inventory of themselves and open up to someone they trust on this issue. On this step, they are guided towards compiling a list of traits and behaviours that have transgressed their moral values. They are also supposed to take an inventory of their "good" traits and the behaviours that represent them. In general, addicts tend to fear this task as it triggers past emotional traumas and reminds them of their past transgressions, which can be quite painful. However, the program enunciates that pain does not only come from acknowledging these character defects, but in fact largely from resisting the process.

Yes, as humans - it is a natural tendency to resist owning up to our own limitations. We instead, prefer to stay safe behind our cloaked identity - even from ourselves. But the first step in true humility is to honestly come to grips with our own shortcomings. If we do not even have the willingness to do this, we could be closing the door to opportunities of growth that we might have never even conceived of.

Also, when one has more awareness of one's strengths and weaknesses - the desire to show off or prove oneself to another also decreases. We are less likely to flaunt how 'clever' we are, what knowledge or accolades we have achieved, or how much 'wealth' we have accumulated. Therefore, it is clear that modesty is simply a by-product of true humility.

In the same light, when we are humbled, not only do we learn more about ourselves but we also become more open to learning from others. Sometimes we forget that all human beings - despite their expertise levels or ages, also have their own valuable experiences, ideals, dreams and lessons. And perhaps even just a small interaction with someone else can really enrich our lives.

> Who knows what we can learn from the smallest of interactions?

A popular Zen saying by Shunryu Suzuki is, "In the beginner's mind there are many possibilities, but in the expert's, there are few."

Looking at it from this angle then, a true sense of humility is actually liberating to the human condition. This is because the incessant need to prove oneself to the world is not only exhausting but also unrewarding in the long-term.

This constant and endless chasing of approval is dangerous, as quoted by Wayne Dyer:

"People who want the most approval get the least and people who need approval the least get the most."

Because being open and vulnerable is a natural transition from humility, with this behaviour also come other perks:

- A more authentic connection with others.
- The ability to remain present and in the flow.
- Increase in energy and as a result of which, creativity flourishes.
- Decrease in anxiety, because of less pressure to 'perform' or fit in.

Lastly, being humble is an attractive quality because it gives us the ability to appreciate others, affirm their behaviours and emotionally nourish the people we are with.

> When we are able to appreciate others and are able to express it openly - it fulfils a part of us that blossoms on seeing others joyful. ➤

In other words, a well-developed sense of humility is thus considered a pre-requisite for 'pro-social behaviour'.

SUMMARY

The bottom line is, humility has nothing to prove, but everything to offer. Practising humility nourishes and empowers us in so many ways:

- Being humble places us in a capacity where **profound self-growth** becomes possible.
- Being open to **learning from others** further serves to enrich our own lives.
- The need to prove oneself diminishes, and we discover a new sense of **personal freedom**.
- Freedom from behaviours linked to external validation, enables our **energies to be diverted** towards inspired action and in alignment with what really matters to us.
- True humility makes us more pleasant to be around with and is crucial to creating more **authentic relationships**.

CHAPTER 5

ALIGNMENT
REMAINING TRUE TO YOURSELF

"The only people who see the whole picture,
are the ones who step outside the frame."
Salman Rushdie

When goals and ambitions take precedence over our lives, there is a risk that we can become overly self-identified and lose sight of our core values. But, what does it really take to step back and recalibrate? This Chapter points us towards a simple path in aligning our goals and value systems, and also some stimulating insight into how our goals can create more meaning in our lives.

Have you ever sat back to imagine *who* you might be 40 years from now? Perhaps you envision that you are on stage receiving a lifetime award for your hard-earned and well-researched scientific paper. Or, maybe you are sitting snuggly in front of a warm fire, in one of your many hotels located all over Switzerland. You might even see yourself retired and living in a beach house, with your grandkids running around you.

No doubt, having SMART goals[47] (specific, measurable, achievable, relevant, time-bound) are imperative to keeping us on track when pursuing our ambitions. Specific goals give us a sense of direction, which also help undercover our innate potential. So in this sense, goals are essential in turning the 'invisible' into the 'visible' - or translating the abstract into the specific. But as Shakespeare once wrote, "All the world's a stage, and all the men and women merely players; they have their exits and their entrances, and one man in his time plays many parts, his acts being seven ages." (How apt was Shakespeare, when it came to nailing down human nature.)

The truth is, we as human beings bring a lot more to the table than the 'roles' we play. What do we mean by this?

All humans possess an extraordinary mental faculty that - unlike any other species in the world - makes us capable of introspection, solving complex problems, and using reasoning to create awareness. Not only this, we are also able to tap into abstract emotions such as freedom, love, bliss and peace - which can transcend all worldly desires.

> **Getting what we 'want' and achieving success, therefore, represents only a small part of us.**

If one were to dig deeper, goals are there to help us fulfil the fashioned roles that we have shaped in order to become 'distinct' in society. The goals we have created for ourselves exist as a sort of 'signature' so we are able to create an exclusivity amongst many others. So, yes - they are important for us to develop our sense of identity and belonging in this world.

But they are only a minute fraction of the real 'you' and 'me'. The 'you' and 'me' that stands for so much more - spiritually, emotionally and morally.

Let's try to step back and contemplate a scenario of which we are completely free of the roles we have today. Let us assume that we are no more representative of our part as 'breadwinner', 'daughter', 'leader', 'politician', 'author', 'businessman', 'teacher', 'entrepreneur', 'parent', etc.

Who would we really be? Looking even deeper - how would our inner child want us to express ourselves? What aspirations and dreams did we have before we were taught the 'meaning' of right and wrong, good or bad, sad and happy?

The only way to really delve into this challenging inquiry is to start digging deep into our value system. Why? Because a concrete value system represents the closest facet to what represents our core nature.

But sometimes as we turn towards our values again, we are also reminded that perhaps we are actually living out of alignment. We realise perhaps that we have lost our sense of real self while on the long trot towards ambition and success. So, what are the signals to pay attention to so we know when we are losing ourselves to ambition?

REDISCOVERING OUR 'WHY'

If you have been feeling jaded about life for some time under pressure to make decisions; enduring sleepless nights; finding yourself constantly stuck between deadlines; suffering from anxiety and overwhelm; or perhaps even feeling numb during times which you should be feeling good – these are just some clear indications that you are losing touch with what is really important to you. This would be the best time right time to halt, re-examine, and re-align.

Here, it is worth pointing out, that taking a step back does not mean you are not turning your back on life. You are merely taking a break to look at what you set yourself out to achieve, and to look at whether it is worth it in the grand scheme of things. Because when we are always rushing to achieve, the most important part of our existence drops– our joy. This situation always reminds me of the saying:

> *You dropped a diamond while you were too busy picking up pennies.*

Quite simply, the diamond represents our presence and enjoyment of life, while our ambitions are embodied by the dozens of pennies. After all, what is the point of living a frazzled existence if we are stuck constantly chasing after something we are not sure we even want? The reality is - this 'chase' is in misalignment with our value systems because our true nature is actually comprised of pure joy and peace. And as a dichotomy, here we find ourselves running away from ourselves.

When examining one's value systems, here are some areas to look into:
- *Our Relationships*
- *Our Health and Body*
- *Our Family Life*
- *Our Work and Career*
- *Our Creative life/Hobbies*
- *Our Spiritual Life*

Here we can reflect on each category, and then list 5 facets of what is most important to us surrounding each of them. It is just that simple. One can draw it out in circles, or have it in a list format. But the key is to keep it visible and close to us on a daily basis.

Drawing out a comprehensive value system helps us reap the powerful benefits of rediscovering our 'why' in life, and enables us to view our lives as a 'whole' picture as opposed to separate fragmented parts.

Because our vision of our future is now clearer, the pressure to achieve in only one area might even slowly begin to chip away.

As a result of this, we find ourselves having more time and energy to introspect and understand what we are doing all of this for. Stepping back also gives us the opportunity to realign ourselves with what it is we really want, which could also even mean a complete revamp of our long term life goals.

At times, some of us are easily influenced by other people's opinions, especially if there is some level of co-dependence or strong emotional connection. But when we find ourselves too emotionally dependent on other people, there begins an unconscious longing for their approval in order for *us* to feel a sense of self-worth. Before we know it - our goals then become tied to other people's expectations of us or what we might perceive them to be.

> But have you ever stopped to even think about your own
> expectations?

Have you looked at your goals in terms of achieving your own values? According to Russ Harris, the author of *The Happiness Trap*, values are "our heart's deepest desires: how we want to be, what we want to stand for, and how we want to relate to the world around us"[48]. He poses these questions:

- Deep down in your heart, what are the things that are most important to you?

- What sort of person do you want to become? What are the things you want to be remembered by?

- What sort of relationships do you want to build and foster? What kind of people do you want around in your life?[49]

Sometimes we become so lost in crossing off goals and to-do tasks off from our lists, that we forget whether they were even aligned to our values in the first place.

For example, if one of your overarching values is to become a more involved parent – your goals would consist of specific steps to become this. You might want to create sub-goals, such as spending quality time during bedtime. Another sub-goal would be to engage in regular conversations with your kids while making it a point to looking into their eyes. Or perhaps another sub-goal would be to collect your child from school 3 times a week.

It is vital for us to draw a distinction because goals and values.

> Our values reflect our lifelong desires or the ongoing inspirations leading us towards the creation of our goals.

Goals, however, are more short-term in nature and can also change according to the circumstances of our value systems.

So, we must look closely at whether our goals and values are calibrated wisely, because connecting with our values provides us with a more consistent and fundamental purpose in life. In other words, our values become the overarching purpose or the 'why' driving our short-term goals.

ONE OF THE SUREST WAYS TO FIND 'YOURSELF'

As a fundamental truth, if your goals involve helping others - they become all the more powerful and end up taking on a momentum of their own. This is because there is nothing that draws you closer to inspiration than human connection and seeing others benefit as a result of your contribution. So, in this sense, you are then more inclined to reach your goals faster.

Mahatma Gandhi once said, "The best way to find yourself is to lose yourself in the service of others." Historically, human beings are actually designed to cooperate and be of service to one another, for the purpose of ensuring survival amongst their tribes or communities. As time has progressed into a more civilised world where survival is taken for granted, helping others also now fulfils an innate need within us. It is a vital instrument in giving us meaning in our lives and a strong sense of self-completion.

In fact, research suggests that when you are engaged in an act of giving a donation or contributing to a charity, your brain acts in a similar way to when you are having sex.[50]

Studies also show that when one engages in helping another, the human body actually releases a hormone called oxytocin. Oxytocin induces feelings of warmth, euphoria and social bonding.

> The joy of being instrumental in someone's happiness is far more powerful than we can possibly imagine.

According to another research study, helping others can also increase one's life expectancy. The University of Buffalo recently found that subjects who provided tangible assistance to friends or family members (running errands, helping with childcare, etc.), reported less stressful events and, consequently, experienced reduced mortality. In other words, "helping others reduced mortality specifically by buffering the association between stress and mortality."[51]

Also, watching others in joyful states - such as a child's smiling face or a cancer survivor's grateful tears - can further induce the intrinsic motivation towards much more evocative depths.

Not long ago, my husband and I were on our usual marathon search for a Netflix series to begin. But then just by chance an advertisement suddenly caught our attention.

A bathroom scene opens with a man brushing his teeth as the tap under him is carelessly left running. A statistic pops up on the screen that we are potentially wasting 6 litres of water per minute.

Then the scene cuts to a cold day in a busy China Town Street. An old and frail man wakes up. He puts on his clothes, leaves his small home and heads to his work. But his work is like no other.

The next scene shows this man in a run-down shelter pouring gallons of steaming water into large-sized cauldrons containing porridge. A sign reads outside '*Serving the Homeless*'. Naturally, the objective of the ad was to juxtapose the two images and display that the same amount of water wasted was enough to feed a large number of homeless people. The message was obviously geared towards urging viewers to save water.

But this was not what drew our attention, (being that we are already highly sensitive to this fact). Instead what captivated us was the powerful unseen message.

Our focus was, instead, towards the old man serving those homeless people every day. We both tried to imagine and conjure up a feeling of how much meaning this man wakes up to every morning. What a privilege it must be to know that he is helping a human being who may not have been alive if it wasn't for his service. What a sense of fulfilment he must be experiencing, knowing he has created a community of people who have bonded over a necessity. And what a pleasure it must be for him to interact with those who were once strangers but have now become authentic connections. And, of course, what a satisfying sentiment he must have to know that people leave his shelter feeling satiated, because he has served them the most basic need of humanity. What could provide a man with more motivation to get out of bed every morning?

Now this was a powerful goal. Beyond any means.

SUMMARY
Goals are designed to help you carve out your roles and provide a structure to your everyday actions, hence also enabling you to have a sense of stability. And because our goals also lead us towards a unique identity within our societies, it is perfectly normal to sometimes feel our goals are driven by external validation. However, it would be helpful to remember that:

- Your goals and achievements do not necessarily **represent what you stand for as a human being**. So be careful not to depend on the success and failure of your goals too much.

- Knowing when to step back from your goals and **recalibrate with your core values** is equally important.
- Intertwining your goal with **volunteer service or acts of goodwill** will provide you with a multitude of benefits.
- **Reflection**: Think about the goals you set for yourself this year. Are they self-serving or beneficial to others as well? Can you find a way to help others with the goal you have set for yourself?

CHAPTER 6

SELF-CARE
PUTTING YOURSELF FIRST

"Rather than being your thoughts and emotions,
be the awareness behind them."
Eckhart Tolle

We've all been there. You walk into your class and overhear a careless comment directed towards you by a well-meaning friend. Minutes later, you are handed your results only to find you have failed your Art Theory finals. And the icing on the cake is as you head towards your local café, you catch sight of your ex-boyfriend walking hand in hand with his new beau. In a snap - possibility suddenly cedes to exist and experiencing pain, we catch ourselves being lead down a cycle of negative thinking. As we are lost in our world of self-pity and despondence, we start to respond much to our own detriment. This may manifest in us doing things which are counteractive to our well-being. Perhaps we may retreat from people we are closest to; find ourselves picking up a cigarette; or even snapping at our loved ones out of frustration. Self-care suddenly goes out the window. And even though we inherently know we are only hurting ourselves further - why do we allow this to happen? This chapter gives us insight into the science of why humans are primed to place so much focus on negative events - especially when there is so much else to be hopeful for. And so it follows - what should we do when we are stuck in a negative loop? For inspiration, there are some quick tips to keeping our spirits elevated when we are feeling low and also some valuable techniques towards long-term, proper self-care.

Oh, how we let our minds control our lives! No stranger to the everyday human psyche, rumination is something that all of us have experienced at some point of our adult lives. What is rumination exactly? Rumination is best described as the constant and persistent fixation on a negative situation. It happens when our minds are swiftly engaged on a constant replay of negative events which perhaps might even involve a varied level of negative self-talk. At times the thoughts can reach a point where it can feel like a broken record, circling over and over in our heads - almost as if no end in sight. But, being that this is a fairly common human tendency, there is a fundamental reason the brain has a large role to play in it.

RUMINATION & OUR BRAIN

It is true that when we engage in any sort of rumination, our mind feels blocked from any rational reasoning. This is largely because the amygdala - the survival centre of our brain - has no choice but to dutifully take over. The amygdala - a very crucial part of our brain - is largely responsible for keeping humans ready to go into 'fight or flight' mode in case of any perceived threats or attack. When this part of the brain is suddenly activated, a large amount of our brain energy moves away from the prefrontal cortex (which is where all cognitive reasoning and rationality is derived from). It then gets diverted towards the amygdala - in order to take quick action, if necessary.

Hereafter, this explains why sometimes we feel 'stuck', when something bad or negative happens to us. Sometimes, we go into a state of 'shock', 'numbness', 'anger', or even 'disbelief'.

> This also explains why there is little possibility for effective problem solving when we are suddenly confronted with an unpleasant situation.

Instead, our minds replay the running reel of the moment that led us to have a horrific outburst on the bus, or how embarrassed we felt when our boss degraded us in front of our colleagues.

Let's dissect what's going on here when we are emotionally (not physically) provoked.

An unpleasant event or comment triggers an upsetting thought in your brain. That thought attaches itself to your sense of self - also commonly referred to as the identity.

Your identity - now feeling threatened, further triggers an uncomfortable emotion to run through your body.

Your body, now incited by an uncomfortable feeling - registers something is wrong, and activates your amygdala to take charge. Now your fight or flight mode is officially on alert. The uncomfortable sensation you felt earlier turns into emotions such as 'anger' or 'shock'. You may even describe this feeling as 'not being able to think straight' (because your prefrontal cortex is not activated anymore).

Because of this trigger, you are more susceptible to a barrage of other upsetting thoughts. And thus, a transmissible cycle is established.

OUR INHERENT NEGATIVE BIAS

Have you ever heard of the expression "down in the dumps"? The process of rumination is just another way of expressing this feeling.

Inherently, one way or another - all adults have experienced feeling low or 'down in the dumps' - some to a larger extent than others. And sometimes, the downward spiral comes on so unexpectedly and our bodies react so quickly - we just are not able to put our finger on exactly what triggered it.

Metaphorically, imagine you are trying to peer through a cloudy fish tank, with sand flying around and fish flurrying around in bouts of excitement. You do not know which particular fish triggered this instant flurry and sudden upheaval - and hence it seems that there is no real start and no real end to the mess.

One could say that one of our primary dispositions to ruminate originates from an inherent trait present in all human beings – known as the 'negativity bias'. This phenomenon states that if presented with a balanced situation, human beings have the tendency to focus primarily on the negative aspects rather than the positive facets. So, even if eight clients walk out of an office ripe with praise, we will tend to hyper-focus on that one surly client who complained about the service. And because the mind can be such a great story-teller, we tend to believe negative propositions such as "I knew I was doing it all wrong", "Screw it - more I was doomed to fail, anyway", "What's the point?", "I'll never truly be happy", and so on.

There is nothing abnormal about this - in fact, research shows that at any one point in time, approximately 80% of our thoughts have some degree of negative content.

But, there is reason to believe that the negativity bias is a well-heeled and necessary phenomenon in our lives, because it's crucial function is to protect us from the danger of extinction. Since the beginning of evolution - our very survival was dependant on our skill of dodging danger. Because of this, our brains needed to hyper-focus on negative input to keep us out of harm's way, and we developed internally reliable systems that would make it impossible for us not to notice signs of danger.

> But today as we live in a much safer world - where tigers are not lurking behind our caves or there are no risks of tribal disruption - psychological triggers such as hurtful comments, rejection and missed opportunities continue to activate our systems in much the same way.

Rick Hanson, PhD and the author of "Hardwiring Happiness" writes so aptly,

"The brain is like Velcro for negative experiences, but Teflon for positive ones."[52]

He describes how the siren of the brain— the amygdala— uses approximately 75% of its neurons to be cautious of bad news. This might help you understand why at times when you are having an exquisite day at work, a harmless critique from your colleague can completely throw you off course!

You might be wondering why understanding this phenomenon, in so much detail, is so important in the grand scheme of things?

It is important to be aware of this, because when we are deep in the midst of a crisis or a cycle of rumination, we can suddenly feel completely alone.

> To make matters worse, science proves that feeling alone in your misery only further exacerbates it.

At times, we forget that even others are experiencing their own hardships, but we don't have access to their worlds because humans are well-accustomed to putting on a brave face for the outside world. The hard truth is that every single human being experiences downward slumps in their life. It is the nature of our evolutionary brain, as you can see. This is also the reason why Facebook, Instagram and other social mediums can create so much deception as they create a false perception and illusion of ingenuine happiness.

Now that we are cognizant of this innate tendency, we need to be keenly aware of our negativity bias when it does crop up. Once we are aware, then we can whole-heartedly accept that this 'negativity bias' is very much an inherent part of the human experience and derive comfort in the fact that others around us are also probably going through the same thing. There is great comfort in knowing that we are definitely not alone. Now that we are mindful of this bias - we have finally crossed the rockiest part of our trail. Now we can find ways to smartly navigate around it, which will help us permanently shift our hardwired negative patterns.

Indeed, there are a number of ways to work through and around a downward slump. But here are three methods targeted towards gradually overcoming a negative frame of mind.

- ***Attention & Awareness***

For starters, remember the Teflon example. Be mindful of the degree to which your survival brain is wired to make you afraid. Some people don't have it to an extreme level but for some, it can be so much so that they walk around with a constant trickle of anxiety (or perhaps even a flood of it).

- ***Practice the 5:1 Method***

Take note of the 5:1 positive to negative ratio. Try to make a conscious effort to **look for** five positive aspects for every one negative experience. Take active measures to notice the good in both the world and yourself. In this sense, you are also practicing being grateful and this act, in turn, will spur up more attractive opportunities. For people unaccustomed to practising this daily, it is recommended to set an alarm on your phone to remind you every few hours, so you can clock in something you feel appreciation for. As you do this, pay attention to any resistance you encounter within yourself and then willingly choose not to focus on it. Practising this at least a half dozen times a day and you can quickly turn it into a healthy habit.

- ***Presence of Mind***

Really learn to attend to positive experiences. While taking a dip into the warm sea or taking that first pleasurable sip of a morning coffee, allow yourself to completely savour and engage in that moment. Sometimes, we do not let ourselves get into that 'good feeling' place because we feel it is a waste of time, or perhaps that we do not deserve it until we have finished our work for the day. But, the idea is to immerse yourself into any good-feeling moment and elongate your positive sensations of the experience. When you focus on what feels good to you, the feelings further solidify into an affirmative experience within your subconscious memory bank.

> And because humans are more predisposed to clinging onto negative thoughts, if we consistently fill up our positive memory bank - the greater our overall life satisfaction will be.

Now, who would not want that?

REWIRING YOUR NEURONS FOR THE BETTER

Now that we have some knowledge on the evolution of the negativity bias and the phenomenon of rumination, we are on our way to learning some techniques to keeping our body and mind healthy for the long haul.

If you ever find yourself in a bit of a rut - it is essential to examine within and check whether your basic needs are being met. For example, are you hungry, thirsty or tired? When one of these basic needs are not balanced or not met at all, we are susceptible to self-destructive behaviours, (rumination, depression, anxiety and the like).

Regulating Your Emotions. When something bad happens to us, our egos get a righteous boost while we drown ourselves in self-pity or blame. Here's the catch. If we are to feel truly content in the present moment, we must pay attention to the emotions we are experiencing. So, do not suppress the emotion - just notice it.

And instead, just give that emotion a name.

> A multitude of research demonstrates that just the mere act of recognizing and labelling your emotions is powerful enough to reduce the effect of the emotion.

When you label your emotions, you switch the brain energy back towards the prefrontal cortex (which as mentioned earlier is the thinking or rational part of the brain). So, you effectively switch the focus away from the survival part of your brain (your amygdala) - towards the rational part of your brain. As a result of this, you can think clearer again and it of course ends up reducing the impact of the emotion.

> The irony here is that sometimes we believe ignoring the emotion will make it 'go away'.

However, studies in neuroscience prove that if we ignore - or are less aware of our emotions - we are then less likely to figure out how to best regulate them! It is similar to that cloudy fish-tank metaphor - where all we see and feel is murkiness.

- So, the first step would be to correctly label it. For example, disappointment, anger, hurt, shyness, nervousness, and so on.

- Secondly, equally important is the art of 'disassociating' the emotion from you – recognising it and labelling it from a third person's perspective. Verbalising as if we are an observer, helps one recognise that those emotions "are not me" and are highly transitory (this term is explained more thoroughly later). An example of this would be saying, "Hey, anger is rising in me now," rather than claiming "I am angry."

- Third, imagine your emotions as 'guests' who come into your home to visit you for a short while. Jelaluddin Rumi, a revered Sufi of his time, aptly wrote centuries ago in his poem 'The Guest House': "This being human is a guest house. Every morning a new arrival. A joy, a depression, a meanness, some momentary awareness comes as an unexpected visitor. Welcome and entertain them all. Even if they are a crowd of sorrows, who violently sweep your house empty of its furniture, still, treat each guest honourably. He may be clearing you out for some new delight."

Step Out of Yourself

I used to see it in my eight-year-old son every morning. He used to wake up in what I call a "me-focused" mood, which would translate into an unusual grumpy and stubborn demeanour. However, considering he is of a highly sentient nature, I figured out a way to snap him out of this mood. So, I would allow the dogs into his room to wake him up, and they would jump on the bed, lick his face or just scratch at the sheets. And it was seriously like a magic veil has been lifted. Suddenly, more important to him than feeling sorry himself, was 'Why is Nala's nose not wet today – is she sick?' or 'Why we haven't brushed the dogs' teeth in so long?' He would in effect, forget his own grumpiness and his tiredness, and would quickly start to get ready for school. Shifting from a "me-focused" attitude to a feeling of concern and love for another being is a wondrous phenomenon because as humans, we are naturally inclined to get distracted by what we love and value.

Therefore, to avoid getting stuck in a "me-focused" frame of mind, which is a recipe for self-deprecation - one of the most profound techniques is to practice 'giving' or being of service to another being. The expression "it is in giving that we receive" rings particularly true here. As we have read in the previous chapter, it is in serving others that we are able to find an important part of ourselves. So, in the deepest midst of a slump, go out there and do something for someone else.

> It doesn't have to be a landslide victory, or something as big as saving someone's life.

Even just the mere act of smiling at or thanking your taxi driver; holding the door open for someone behind you; picking up a littered piece of trash lying on the road or signing up for a charitable cause - is enough to pull us out of a "me-focused" mind-set. The motive does matter: if you are trying to support more than just yourself, you are able to feel a sense of community and can connect better with other beings. And that forms a huge part of our most basic needs - a sense of belonging - to a bigger and more profound existence than just ourselves.

People really tend to underestimate the power of having a systematic self-care routine. We are so easily drawn straight into our email inboxes, work calls or social media from the minute we wake up. But without a complete mind-body haul up every day, we are missing the ingredients of a long-term satiating life experience. Why? Because what we need to remain consistently feeling stable and content is a set of daily routines to keep our minds and bodies in good synergy. A simple way of ticking all the self-care boxes is by committing oneself to the three daily criteria below:

Moving the Body

Whether it be a kick-boxing class; dancing with wild abandon in the comfort of your room; or a quick run up one flight of stairs - exercise is an immediate miracle worker. The benefits of exercise are known to induce and increase those 'feel-good' chemicals in our brains, reduce stress hormones and even help relieve anxiety. An even bigger boost is to move your body somewhere in nature, also known as "forest therapy". Moreover, the effects of exercise or a sudden prolonged burst of movement, lasts for 12 hours.

Breathing (Accompanied by Meditation)

A deep breath activates the body's natural relaxation response by stimulating a part of our body, known as our Para-sympathetic Nervous System (PNS). The PNS is responsible for activities that occur when our body is at rest. It functions in an opposite manner to the Sympathetic Nervous System, which stimulates activities associated with the fight-or-flight response. Some people wonder why simple meditation (a concentrated state of mind) is best done after deep breathing exercises. The reason behind this is that meditation becomes easier and much more effective when the mind and body are primed to be relaxed.

Daily Spiritual Reading

Engaging with a daily spiritual reader or keeping up with prayer is so essential to keeping you in tune with the natural order of the world. Just one page of a book can pull you out of transitory pleasures and pains, and remind you that you are much bigger than the issues you face.

> We are also reminded that emotions are forever changing.

They continuously ebb and flow, from mild to intense, from blissful to dreary, from unexpected to the pleasant. Awareness of this helps to accept and embrace our current situation, despite what we might be going through, good or bad. Through prayer, we are able submit ourselves to a higher power - which is so necessary for our well-being.

Stimulate your Brain: Novel Experiences

Lastly, an additional bonus boost to our well-being comes from involving ourselves in a new or novel experience. Whether this means watching a National Geographic documentary; starting a new collection of stamps; or even jumping onto a rollercoaster for the first time - the idea is to keep ourselves mentally stimulated and in a state of constant flow.

In fact, learning something new can uplift our spirits greatly. Studies show that every time we engage in a novel experience, our body gets a rush of the reward chemical - dopamine. This new flow of dopamine in our blood also is a great distraction to what has caused us to experience pain in the first place - an auxiliary detractor to rumination. Furthermore, learning new things or conducting challenging tasks keeps your brain young, as new information helps build connections between neurons, (replacing some of those we lose over time.)

SUMMARY

The Negativity Bias is a very real phenomenon and is evolutionarily set to protect us from experiencing danger. (Remember the Teflon example - how our brains are wired to protect us.)

> **No wonder human beings are primed to focus on the negative!**

When you find yourself in a slump or a cycle of rumination, also remember that you are in no way alone. Also, over time one can gradually work around this tendency, through recognising that it is completely normal to feel low at times. Also, by practicing acceptance and gratitude daily and immersing oneself into the present moment - one can help rewire these negative hardwired patterns.

There are also some robust tools to keep you emotionally resilient when you find yourself stuck in a negative loop:

- Learning how to disassociate with your negative feelings through the act of **'labelling your emotions'**.
- Practicing **stepping outside of yourself**, and instead focusing on any outside cause, person or being.
- Sticking to a daily **3 Step routine**: exercise, meditation (breathing), and prayer/spiritual reading. One can try to keep a spiritual reading or audio accessible in close range - whether in a handbag, car, bedside table or at your workplace.
- **Learning something new** or keeping yourself inspired is a huge benefactor in priming your mind towards more interesting stimuli, rather than the events that have led you to feel down.

CHAPTER 7

AWARENESS
TUNING INTO YOUR INNER FIELD

"When you find peace within yourself, you become the kind of person who can live at peace with others."
Peace Pilgrim

The human endeavour towards perfection is more of a curse than a blessing. Looking back a decade ago, I can envisage a running reel of myself working in blind fervour to be the trophy wife, mother and business woman. Success was always just around the corner, and I was perpetually just one step away from it. But this is when life started to go 'south', and before I knew it, a sense of overwhelm began to take over my every move as I strived towards doing everything that was expected of me. Many a times, I was well aware that I was disrespecting the limitations of my body. But the smell of success was just too sweet to let go of. And because of the undeniable link between body and mind - anxiety started to infiltrate every area of my life. Some mornings I would wake up drenched in a cold sweat, steadying myself constantly to a restless heartbeat. Other days, I would find myself perusing through a supermarket, legs buckling with a sudden dizzy urge to sit down. In exchange for superwoman status, a steady lack of internal cohesion started to eventually take over and over time I sadly recognised that I was no longer in control over my bodily reactions anymore. In the following chapter, we examine how one can avoid slipping into this very real phenomenon known as anxiety. Here we will be learning the secrets of how to pay attention to the signals expressed by our most special gift - our bodies.

A month before I hit my 30th birthday, I was diagnosed by a psychotherapist as having General Anxiety Disorder (GAD). I had futilely ignored all the signs - nauseating tightness in my stomach; heart palpitations; dizziness in big crowds; and constant spots lurking in my left eye anytime I felt nervous.

Until one night, I lay myself down on the bed to sleep, and suddenly lost complete control of my lower body. Without any warning, my back started to uncontrollably quiver and twitch all the way from the back of my lower spine, towards my lower abdomen and down the legs towards my toes. This continued not just for a few minutes, but rather a few hours. As my parents and husband rushed me straight to the closest emergency room, the quivering proceeded to get worse. What was happening to me? I wondered. The worst possible scenarios started flooding my mind. 'Maybe I had some incurable disease that the doctors would not be able to cure.' Then another chilling thought hit - and another until suddenly, my emotions began spiralling out of control.

The panic only continued to worsen and soon I could barely breathe. It was only when the perplexed night nurse in the emergency room injected a mild relaxant into a drip, did the quivering gradually begin to subside. And, it was only then that my husband and I grasped that this severe bodily reaction had much more to do with the mind - and much less to do with the body. What I learnt later on after a series of MRI and ultrasound tests, was that I had suffered from a very severe anxiety attack. The doctors claimed that it was most likely due to a culmination of extraordinarily high stress levels over some time to which I had finally succumbed.

But, one will never know what life's plan has in store for us. And this is most likely why this terrifying period of my life was also my biggest and blessed warning.

> **It was a clear signal of how I urgently needed to take care of myself and my body.** ❦

Because of the deep scar that anxiety had left on my being, I knew I had to reverse the trend and a whole overhaul of mind-set and self-care finally met its union in my everyday life. And now, almost a decade later - the rewards of self-compassion have reaped so many benefits. Most importantly, a deep acceptance has set in - embracing that I can be good enough without having to be perfect at everything I do. (This being said, it was definitely not an easy feat to unlearn all those conditioned and unrealistic expectations I had put on myself.)

GETTING BACK IN TOUCH WITH OUR BODY

Our body is constantly sending us signals all the time through the carrier of emotions. At any one point in time, we could be revelling through feelings such as peace, elation, excitement, freedom, clarity, and love. At others, we could be drudging through sensations such as dread, discomfort, exhaustion, over stimulation and fatigue. When we are in a state of feeling 'good' or are experiencing the former type of emotions, our body feels in natural alignment with our inner being. Our inner being is the purest source of our energy, the non-physical part of our being - some like to call it our soul or our God force. When we are in alignment with our inner being, we are overwhelmed with a feeling of well-being which we cannot explain. It is believed that our true nature and inner being is made of pure bliss and love, and that is the natural state of how we came onto this earth.

But nowadays, there are many interferences and distractions that block us from recognising these very poignant signals. With today's electronic bombardment of constant mental stimulation and an ever-ready influx of information at our fingertips - we are actually duped into believing that what is happening outside ourselves takes more precedence to what is happening within. As we gradually lose contact with our internal states, we slowly become immune (if not ignorant) to the body's vital messages. And eventually, when the body gives up and disease takes over…we blame our body for not warning us.

We forgot to tune in and pay attention to these important signals. We forgot how to re-align ourselves with our palpable internal states, just as a baby does when they are hungry, tired or scared. We allowed ourselves to get distracted. Here we learn some powerful techniques to help realign ourselves back with this very precious gift known as 'life'.

THE PARADOX OF GOING GENTLE

Once upon an 'anxious time', going on holiday for me would put into motion an unequivocal amount of excessive planning. Planning for some might mean having a rough itinerary of what they wanted to do in a new place. But in my world, planning equated to efficiency and being efficient meant I needed excel sheets. These excel sheets led my family and me towards the most jaw-dropping adventures and experiences but also transcended into lots of lists and stressful time-bound tasks. (In fact, a standard holiday for our family was once sub-categorised into Date, Time, Location, Contact Person and Activity, and - well, you get the picture.)

On a particular family holiday back to my native place of birth, I had the pleasure of spending some quality time with my cousin. Not only is she one of the most beautiful souls I have ever been in contact with, she also happens to be a world-renowned Breathing Expert and Meditation teacher. She was to sit with me and teach me some beneficial relaxation techniques, in between the controversial excel sheet list of things to do! Midway through our series of breathing exercises, I found my thoughts begin to divert. Realising that dinner had not been organised for the kids and they had to eat within the hour, I started to panic and could steadily feel the palpitations setting in. (Folks, this is what it was like in the day in the life of an anxious person.) I shuffled and shifted around - feeling my heartbeat raise a bit. Ping! My internal anxiety siren went off:

"Why am I not able to just relax, for once?"

Just in that quick gap of consciousness, my cousin gently prodded my shoulder and my eyes slowly opened to meet her kind brown eyes. It was pure synchronicity that she had actually been sharp enough to catch me in the throes of my anxiety.

She smiled understandingly and proceeded to demonstrate a technique of gently breathing in and out of the nose "just like a rose". I watched her as she gently emulated a breathing movement with a nod of her head, letting a barely audible deep breath escape her lips.

Her movements were simple… just like a rose. Simple, unassuming, gentle, easy… I realised then, that even a breath - responsible for our entire life force - can be just as simple as that.

The truth was, all this time, I was clearly not aware of my tense state as I regularly breathed in and out throughout my day. This imbalance of breath plays a key role on our state of mind, and hence must have been causing more stress and unintended havoc on my nervous system.

We are taught that in order to relax, we must take deep and long breaths. But the irony is, no one teaches us how to do so. So, we strain, we push, we pull, we hold in, and we inevitably tense up. But when we strain our breath like this, our muscles also paradoxically end up tightening up too. And this lands up causing us to feeling even more stressed than we were in the first place.

Of course, because breathing is our most natural movement, it should most definitely not be a stressful experience. When muscles tighten from stress, they are part of a primitive physiological reflex that puts the body on guard, alerting any danger.

> This is also known as 'emotion-bound' muscle tension, which plagues many people without them even being aware of it.

If we think about it, how many times a day do we really pay attention to whether our bodies and muscles are relaxed or tensed?

This push and pull movement turns into a vicious circle. The mind causes the body to tense up, and conversely, the tense body and breath causes the mind to remain on high alert. But the good news is we can correct it at both levels.

This sudden awareness of body and muscle tension, and constant 'push and pull' phenomenon started to become more visible and infiltrate almost every aspect of my life. Putting the kids to bed; hailing a taxi; having a casual conversation with a good friend; writing a blog post; preparing my gym bag – a tense body pervaded almost every part of my day. As this mysterious phenomenon started unravelling itself to me, a poignant question befell in my mind

'How come I had never noticed this before?'

As if hit by a ton of bricks, I suddenly had the realisation that I needed to start paying more attention to my body and breath (even during what seemed the most trivial of moments.)

> I simply just needed to slow down.

In the ancient Tantric scriptures, there is a process known as *Yoga Nidra* - which is where one consciously relaxes each part or area of the body, while in a lying down position. In fact, some people use it before going to sleep as a form of relaxation. And then there are others which do it at the end of a yoga sequence to relax. This concept of a 'body scan' intrigued me, and I actively started to practice it when alone having a meal, at my desk working or in bed before sleep. What I noticed is it would take me minutes for my mind to really settle down and be able to focus on each area. But after a while, as I started actively incorporating this quick body scan or 'check-in' into my daily routine, I recognised my body was never quite completely relaxed. Even while doing the most mundane of tasks - I would catch my lower stomach muscles tighten, my fingers clench, or my neck stiffen up. Immediately, I knew it was a sign I was not doing something right. So, even something as basic as how we breathe or whether our bodies are relaxed - makes a huge impact on how we will go through our day.

THE SECRET OF BECOMING MORE PRESENT

We hear about the importance of being present in the moment but how do we incorporate this sense of presence in our daily lives? It's simple. Besides being aware of our breath and body, we can also do this by slowing down all our movements.

For example, instead of rushing through our meals, we can learn to reduce our pace and instead make a conscious effort to taste each bite of food that is on our plate. (We will remember our meals a whole lot better if we enjoy the moments in between each bite.) Or, instead of running to the car to check if the headlights are still on, we can make a conscious attempt to walk more deliberately, enjoy the breeze against our skin, and not just hear - but really listen to the birds singing.

> Do you find as you get older, the years feel closer together?

Focusing on the present moment and actively engaging all our five senses in everything that we do, is actually proven to elongate our memories and help slow down the pace of our lives. I have a theory that the reason my short-term memory is so depraved is because the multitasker in me is always rushing to get to the next crucial moment of the day!

For instance, there are moments where I obliviously toss my house keys into my handbag while attending to an important conference call. Then, for the rest of the day, I presume that I have lost my keys while actually it was sitting in my bag the whole day long. My brain does not think that such trivial acts are important enough to remember, so instead it moves towards and pays attention to the next important task. But the actuality of slowing down and paying attention to each moment is that it helps us focus; helps us remember things (especially for the multi-tasker in us); be more mindful and maintain a more peaceful state of mind. So, it is completely necessary to slow down even for those 'small, trivial things'.

When you consciously relax and allow yourself to fully immerse into every situation, you start to become more aware of what is actually happening around you. You will automatically pick up on 'simple things' such as what you took for granted but are immensely grateful for, like the texture of your dog's fur; the sound of running water; or the texture and sweetness of a warm apple pie. Also, when one is fully engaged and present - he or she is also able to pick up people's non-verbal signals with more accuracy and can easily sense when a situation is not going well. As you do things slowly and give it your complete attention - you also consciously engage the different sounds, sights, feelings, tastes, and smells of your sensory system. This is when your instinct becomes truly alive and you miraculously find yourself being able to tap into situations with more focus and clarity. **If you ask me - this is the true act of meditation - when you are able to bring your presence to the outside world, not just in a quiet environment.**

KEEPING THINGS SIMPLE

Many of us still believe that our intrinsic worth as a human being comes from being a 'doer' - from having to constantly be achieving something worth-while or by constantly being busy with 'things' that fill up our day. Nowadays, this phenomenon has aptly been termed as the disease of 'being busy', and the backlash is viable. The thought process is something like this:

I am only worth something if I am constantly doing something.

And then, of course, there are those of us who grow up taking life in our stride and just focusing on one day at a time. But for those of you who are the doers, during the days that are busy, loud and vexing to your well-being - the key is to just stop. Stop and in fact, move slower than usual. Here, one can cut things out and only do what is completely necessary on our priority lists.

> In fact, the busier the day gets, the easier we must go on our self.

When life becomes too chaotic for us to keep up with, it is natural for us to lose track of what is really important in our day and what actually needs our immediate attention. In other words, we really can benefit by making things as simple as possible by taking a moment to set our priorities.

It could mean we could streamline our appointments, cancel what is not necessary and just focus on the things that feel good to us. I make it a principle not to keep more than three major activities per day on my schedule. It is essential for me to do this, considering I easily fall prey to stress and overwhelm. Even if it means saying 'no', one must do what is necessary to keep one's own serenity in balance. One can also ask themselves

"What's the worse that will happen if I can't do it all?"

LEARNING HOW TO CHECK IN

Mastering how to tap into our bodily rhythm throughout the day also enables us to become more present. This means one could be actively taking note of the body - observing the shoulders, stomach, breathing, forehead tension, and how the fingers are placed. In natural course, once one becomes accustomed to checking into the body every few hours, the mind will unconsciously adjust to this new habit. Now because I am so accustomed to 'checking in', my body miraculously starts alerting me if it is not completely at ease. Anytime I catch myself biting on my inner cheek, or I wake up in the mirror see a line creased across my forehead - it is a clear signal to me something is bothering me.

If this practice is new to you, you can ask yourself:

Are you feeling relaxed in all areas of your body? (Move up slowly from the toes towards the head)

Are you paying attention to the areas where you usually get tense?

If so, what can you do to ease the discomfort? (Move around, stretch, deep breaths etc…)

If you sit in front of your laptop throughout the majority of your day, you might feel the need to observe your neck and shoulder areas. If you are often stuck behind the wheel in traffic, take this opportunity to feel your feet, legs and thighs - and perhaps stretch them from time to time to release any tension. If you are a student sitting through a big exam or test, you can pay attention to the muscles in your stomach, and if they are tense - practice breathing deeply for release.

As we already know by now, the body and mind work as a unified entity. This implies that lurking behind any type of body or muscle-bound tension, there could also very well be something more profound going on in the mind. This can be a reflection of disappointment with someone's behaviour; a sign of pressure to achieve something; or a cascade of negative thoughts taking over.

Osho says in his book *Body Mind Balancing*:

"A person who has been suppressing anger, his jaw becomes locked. All the anger comes up to the jaw and then stops there. His hands become ugly. They don't have the graceful movements of a dancer; that is because anger flows into the fingers—and they become blocked. Remember, anger has two sources to be released from. One is teeth, another is fingers. If you suppress anything, in the body, there is some part, a corresponding part, to the emotion."[53]

The reality is, any sense of dissatisfaction indicates to us that we are resisting what life is offering to us at that very moment. For this reason, it would be wise to pay attention to our body's signals and assess whether we are in resistance mode or simply allowing life to flow towards us. Of course, this is much easier said than done, but tapping into this is so vital for our long-term wellbeing. Why? Because when the body keeps getting the signal that we are under threat (i.e., in resistance mode), the stress hormone cortisol will become a regular visitor to our bodies to help counteract the 'stress' response. Elevated cortisol levels secreted over a long time eventually leads the body towards anxiety and burnout.

STOP. AND SET YOUR INTENTION.

Before you begin any major task or project which might instil fear in you, make it a point to 'set the stage' by a written or verbal intention. For instance, if you have a fear of public speaking and you have been requested to give a talk to a group of investors - you might want to set an intention to feel relaxed and confident as you step onto stage.

Here is a simple visualisation technique for those who are fearful of speaking in front of crowds:

Close your eyes.

Begin to visualise what you will be wearing on the day of your speech, the expression on your face, and an upright body stance. Imagine yourself walking confidently onto stage while you are secretly smiling within because you know you are going to be delivering valuable information. As you begin speaking, you feel yourself actually feeling peaceful, relaxed and in the flow. The words are pouring out naturally and you are magically coming up with more creative ideas as you speak. As you embrace this feeling of confidence, you realise how easy it is to speak to this group. You recognise that the investors are feeling empathetic towards you and are listening with respect and interest. In fact, speaking to them is almost as easy as talking to your family members over the dinner table. It's easy, and you find yourself really relaxed. And because you are relaxed, the audience is also relaxed, because that's the universal law of human nature. People reflect the energy we emit. As you wind up your speech, you feel a sense of satisfaction run up your body. You possess a sudden surge of inspiration and gratitude towards the group in front of you. You leave the stage feeling light and clear - ready to meet everyone to discuss the next steps.

You can use this kind of visualisation process with anything that you would like to set an intention for. In fact, if you prefer to recall facts or think in visual images, then it might even be useful to choose a metaphor or a visual symbol to embody the right behaviour. This will enable your mind to mirror the behaviour more accurately. So, setting an intention coupled with a visualisation process, is the most sure-shot route to achieving your outcome, especially if you suffer from the nerves.

REFRAMING 'THE IDEA' OF A PERFECT LIFE

While narrating your exciting weekend to the office gang and your colleague cuts you off mid-conversation - you lose your cool and throw him a dirty look.

Stranded in a busy train station, your friend stands you up and does not bother to message - you react by sending a nasty message.

Your book is delayed by a year - you decide to throw in the towel.

It is clear. Life does not and will not always work in your favour. But instead of subjecting ourselves to high stress levels or engaging in resistance against people and circumstances - we have the remarkable ability to reframe our mind-set. These three reframing strategies can be helpful when you feel that life is just not going your way, and there is nothing you can do about it:

Practice Compassion for Yourself

We must learn to let go of the guilt that is attached to us making mistakes and not getting things done to the 'T'. At times, we might foolishly respond to a situation; or act out of haste and lose out on an opportunity; or react and lose ourselves to anger. But forgiveness towards ourselves is imperative, because the way we respond to life depends on the skills we have at the time; the frame of mind we are in; and how we perceive the situation based on our past experience.

Simply said, we are always doing the best we can with whatever resources we have available to us. It could be that at the time, we did not have as much objectivity or acted out of a survival instinct. If we remember to think kind thoughts toward ourselves and show ourselves some compassion - we can move on gracefully instead of remaining stuck in old patterns. If we can learn to think of ourselves as our own ally, speak to ourselves with love and kindness and put ourselves first on the priority list - being gentle will flow naturally. Remember: "To err is human; to forgive, divine." Let's learn to forgive ourselves first - perhaps by even speaking to ourselves as if we would to our own child.

It's okay to lose control sometimes.

In the same light, there's only so much planning and strategising one can do. And there is only so much control we can have over other people's actions and circumstances. When we find ourselves stuck in rumination mode, it would be wise to pause and examine the things that we can control. In a metaphorical sense, we may not be able to prevent a storm from hitting us but we definitely can be prepared for it. In the same way, we may not be able to control other people's behaviour or actions, but we can control our own reaction to them. Most of the time, when people behave wrongly towards us, we stand to benefit by remembering to not take it personally.

> Because more often than not, their behaviour is a reflection of what has been triggered within them. Not us.

Trust Divine Timing

Each time you tell yourself, "I will only be happy once 'X' happens," you close the door on valuable lessons or on the other ways that your life could be filled with pleasure. Be open to what comes your way - even if it's not the gala invite you expected; or the salary rise you wanted; or the relationship you dreamed of. Say 'yes' to what you have already and stay in gratitude for 'what is'. Open your mind up to the idea that the right things will happen when the time is right for you, and the more we try to force situations or people- the more we are fighting against the natural order of the world.

SUMMARY

If we are not accustomed to tapping into our body's internal signals, we can never master the precious human gift of awareness. And more often than not, when we put ourselves under too much pressure - we fall victim to forgetfulness, anxiety, stress, chronic depression and a lack of enjoyment of life. If your days are in a constant stream of things to do and you are buckling under the pressure of it all, here are some specific techniques to avoid falling further down this slippery slope:

- **Deliberately Slow Down Your Movements.** Take the proper amount of time to savour and enjoy every moment (i.e., mindful mealtime, or walking slowly to your next appointment).

- **Keep Things Simple.** Streamline cut out and simplify your day to only the high priority things you really need to do. A bonus would be to make sure at least one of them is self-care related. Leave everything else out, even if that means you end up sitting on your sofa pouring over a magazine. It's fine.

- **"Checking In".** Paying attention to each part of your body might seem counter-intuitive at first, but this is a fantastic gateway to teaching yourself to become more present.

- **Setting an Intention Before A Big Task.** Choosing a metaphor or a visual image that embodies your behaviour will help your mind mirror the correct conduct.

- **Reframing Your Perspective.** By practising self-compassion; letting go of the need to control other people and circumstances; and trusting divine timing - we can ease out the anxiety that comes with living a high-pressure life.

Chapter 8

Acceptance
Resilience through Pain

"New beginnings are often disguised as painful endings".
Lao Tzu

In life, we all inevitably come face to face with different levels of hardship, struggle and pain. Perhaps one has experienced the betrayal of a long-term partner who has found someone else. Or one is struggling to deal with a life-changing rehabilitating injury. Whatever it may be - human suffering is very much a tangible part of life and as much as we try, we simply cannot avoid it. But living in resistance to 'what is' will always remain to be an exercise in futility - and it is in this very resistance where our biggest struggles lie. Instead, with steadfast faith and trust - we can be led to believe that underneath every 'good' or 'bad' situation beckons a silver lining which serves for everyone's greater good. Not only this, how can we stand to benefit from the pain we are experiencing? What virtues does it provide us with? How will it help us grow? What new paths can it bring us? This chapter helps us to work through a set of skilful ideologies, so we can take advantage of struggle as an opportunity for self-transformation. And when we are able to truly embrace this, we are then able to ride through the rough times with an attitude of grace and acceptance. I like to call it my secret formula for living

A few years ago, I was invited to give a motivational talk for a group of thirty five brave ladies, all of whom had recently come out of a series of life-threatening acid attacks. I was informed by the organizer that some of these ladies had completely stopped going out in public because they were experiencing a sense of humiliation due to their scarred faces and bodies. If this wasn't bad enough, a lot of them had also lost hope and motivation to support their own families, which was unviable considering the socio-economic background they were from. Unlike any other talks I had ever done in the past, many restless nights were spent probing on how to unwrap this severe ordeal for them. How could I inspire them to go back out into the world and start a fresh life again? As much as I tried to find inspiration within, the words were not pouring out - at least not from my heart.

Then by some providential intervention, I happened to be attending a conference during that period in time, and one of the speakers happened to speak about 'change' and metamorphosis in our lives. It went like this:

"A man found a cocoon of a butterfly, that he brought home. One day a small opening appeared in the cocoon. He sat and watched the cocoon for several hours as the butterfly struggled to force its body through that little hole. Then it seemed to stop making progress. It appeared as if the butterfly had gotten as far as it could, and it could go no further. The man decided to help the butterfly in its struggle. He took a pair of scissors and snipped off the remaining bit of the cocoon…and the butterfly emerged easily.

As the butterfly emerged, the man was surprised. It had a swollen body and small, shrivelled wings. He continued to watch the butterfly expecting that, at any moment, the wings would dry out, enlarge and expand to support the swollen body. He knew that in time the body which would contract, and the butterfly would be able to fly.

But neither happened!

In fact, the butterfly spent the rest of its life crawling around with a swollen body and shriveled wings.

It was never able to fly.

What the man, in his kindness and haste, did not understand was that the restricting cocoon and the struggle were required for the butterfly to be able to fly. The butterfly must push its way through the tiny opening to force the fluid from its body and wings. Only by struggling through the opening, can the butterfly's wings be ready for flight once it emerges from the cocoon.

The lesson here is sometimes struggles are exactly what we need in our life. If God allowed us to go through our life without any obstacles, it would cripple us. We would not be as strong as what we could have been.

And we could never fly."[54]

As my heart drummed over the last sentence, I knew right then that this was the perfect metaphor I could provide to the ladies.

Of course, most humans are primed to avoid pain because evolutionarily, 'pain' is equated with 'death'. But how do most people deal with pain? Some live in denial their whole lives, and keep the pain buried away - only for it to come back to life one day in full vengeance. Others become angry and bitter - and keep the injustice alive in their everyday actions. Some live in self-pity and regret, and gain satisfaction from blaming others.

But as I was preparing my talk, a poignant realisation dawned upon me. It may not be that we need to really avoid pain and struggle - like most humans are primed to do. Rather, if we could simply reframe the way we think of pain and suffering in our life - we could really stand to benefit in many ways. **If we looked at suffering as a road leading to a higher purpose or a more meaningful destination, there could be so many ways we could play with a 'bad' situation.**

On the day itself, as I wrapped up the talk - I looked up at a sea of blank faces and was engulfed by a peculiar silence in the room. A flood of thoughts took over.

Did they understand the point of the story? Was my English too fast? Perhaps they were bored.

And then slowly some chairs started to move and squeak against the wooden floor. And as the women stood up to re-join their friends, a certain liveliness took over the room. Suddenly the small hall was abounding with the sound of animated chatter. When mingling with them all later, I learnt many of them were eagerly talking about setting up support groups or looking for ways to work with those who had also suffered from the same ordeal. Of course, I was elated.

In the *Journal of Humanistic Psychology*, a study was conducted on individuals who had experienced bouts of intense turmoil and trauma in their lives. The participants had experienced either intense upheaval; depression; serious illness; impairment; addiction; or even brief encounters with death.

> Yet despite all the hardship, it appeared that these individuals had experienced positive psychological transformation following the turmoil.

After in-depth interviews with the participants, they were then assessed on what were the most prevalent characteristics of their "new state of being"[55]. What they found was that these individuals had a new sense of "increased well-being; intensified perception; a sense of connection; improved relationships; a less materialistic and more altruistic attitude…and a reduced fear of death."[56]

As I flipped through the results of the studies, I wondered about the 'gift' of hardship these people had received. What were the headways leading them from such a state of extreme misery to this new and positive state of being?

It turns out that the results of this psychological transformation largely came from two factors:

- The participants' ability to detach themselves from psychological attachments played a large role in helping them overcome their respective ordeals.

- The participants' ability to practice acceptance during the time when they felt the most pain.

OUR BIGGEST STRUGGLE: LETTING GO

In the *Four Noble Truths* Buddha teaches us that suffering is naturally inherent in every living being. He, in fact, ascertains that the real cause of an individual's suffering has not so much to do with the situation itself, but more to do with the way our minds respond to certain phenomena. That is to say, if we are habituated towards resistance of 'what is', we are only pitting ourselves against the natural order of life and that is ironically where the real suffering takes place. As Eckhart Tolle rightly says,

> "The primary cause of unhappiness is never the situation but thought about it. Be aware of the thoughts you are thinking. Separate them from the situation, which is always neutral. It is as it is."

How does this show up in our lives? Resistance comes in many forms. Some like to revel in the 'unfairness of life' and claim back their power by wallowing in self-pity. Some of us gain comfort by escaping and this might manifest in unhealthy habits, such as smoking or overeating. And there are those who seek solace by looking for modes of revenge and vengeance. It is no wonder this apparent lack of acceptance and overarching sense of resistance is often one of the biggest bones of contention I face with my clients. During one such coaching session, a client exclaimed: "I don't get it - if acceptance is like giving up on trying to improve your situation, then isn't that being passive?"

She had a point, no doubt. From a highly pragmatic viewpoint, we are conditioned in our earlier years to believe that to succeed in life - we must "never give up".

But extensive research on the topic shows that "passiveness" is, in fact, quite the opposite of "acceptance". Psychologist Jon Kabat-Zinn, founder of the 'Center for Mindfulness in Medicine, Health Care, and Society', explains:

"Acceptance doesn't, by any stretch of the imagination, mean passive resignation. Quite the opposite. It takes a huge amount of fortitude and motivation to accept what is – especially when you don't like it – and then work wisely and effectively as best you possibly can with the circumstances you find yourself in and with the resources at your disposal, both inner and outer, to mitigate, heal, redirect, and change what can be changed."[57]

My Secret Formula for Acceptance: V.A.I.S.O

Even though we all endure different types of challenges in our lives, pain does entail a tussle with the human mind and heart. But while we cannot control what happens to us from the outside, we can most definitely work on ourselves. In fact, if we can reframe our attitude towards the concept of suffering, then in the wake of this - we can even derive a meaningful purpose. Here is one simple formula, V.A.I.S.O, to help one work through any type of challenging set-back:

VIRTUE: What virtues can this situation help me to practice so I can become more resilient and a better human being?

"Anything that annoys you is teaching you patience. Anyone who abandons you is teaching you how to stand up on your own two feet. Anything that angers you is teaching you forgiveness and compassion. Anything that has power over you is teaching you how to take your power back. Anything you hate is teaching you unconditional love. Anything you fear is teaching you courage to overcome your fear. Anything you can't control is teaching you how to let go."
-Jackson Kiddard

> Every blunder, every painful moment, every missed chance - they all give us a chance to practice really valuable virtues.

These moments in time can provide us opportunities so one can further cultivate virtues such as calmness, grace, strength, courage, compassion, patience and resilience amongst many others.

To cite an example, I recently underwent an excruciatingly painful tooth abscess, which had actually reached the bone of my gum. As I lay in bed in the middle of the night, I patiently waited for the opioids prescribed by the hospital doctor to kick in and give me some relief. But the agony was so intense - even the strongest pain killer would not work. Left with no external solution to bear me through the night, I knew at this point that I could only use my inner tools. At this point it must have been 2am. As I was peering over at the back of my spouse's head, who was clearly exhausted, I could see he was googling on ways to heal tooth pain. I suddenly felt so much gratitude. Closing my eyes, I gave thanks to the universe for gifting me such a caring man.

This feeling of gratitude led me to think about how much stronger I would be the next day after the root canal surgery. I imagined the exhilaration of cycling my way through my spin class, revelling in the dark room, listening to the pounding beats, and sweating out all the toxic medication. I imagined the liberation I would feel after the class was over. This 'future gain' gave me something to look forward to the next day - and also the patience and strength to bear through the night. Although the physical pain did not heed much, the shift in mind-set kept my resilience strong until the next morning. Although this is an example of a temporary (physical) incident - in these times too, one can practice virtues to help us become resilient and build character.

ADJUST: What can I do to help me adjust better to the situation?

From the Buddhist perspective, all human beings are endowed with the innate ability to adjust to any situation - no matter how awful or tragic. Similarly, the great Roman Emperor, Marcus Aurelius, wrote: "Our actions may be impeded…but there can be no impeding our intentions or dispositions. Because we can accommodate and adapt. The mind adapts and converts to its own purposes the obstacle to our acting."[58] After all, we wouldn't be human if we couldn't change, as life is one of constant change and reinvention.

We are also lucky in this lifetime to have discovered the remarkable phenomenon of neuroplasticity - which shows us that our behaviours and ways of thinking are not fixed. In fact, our brain cells are continuously forming new connections and restructuring our perceptions over time.

Hence we now know, with scientific and biological evidence, that we can easily rewire the way we respond to outside events. What this means is that trauma does not have to make such a resounding impact to our current situation, nor does it have to remain in our brain forever. We can consciously work on this through practicing exercises and activities which effectively help reroute our memories and neuron activity. How? Some people might turn to mindfulness exercises; hypnotherapy; meditation or Cognitive Behavioural Therapy (CBT). Some might even learn a new sport or a new language. The point is - whatever you choose to do and practice consistently, will eventually help your brain form new connections and possibly even act as a useful distraction from the situation.

Some might even feel better by spending time with people they admire or feel affiliated to. This is because spending time with those who are oriented towards a particular way can help rewire the way we think, and hence, act.

By a psychological process known as transference - when one spends a considerable amount of time with someone else - their ways of thinking and their modes of language actually start to 'rub off' on the other.

In effect, the person ends up becoming remarkably similar to the other, as they absorb much of what the other person knows and practices.

You might observe this phenomenon at the end of a spiritual retreat. The positive energy and union does not occur just because of what one has imbibed through the course - but also largely due to the group of individuals who have spent days, hour and minutes together. Having experienced this phenomenon myself, I can easily describe it as a miraculous synergy of people taking place. Because our brains have adjusted to new or similar patterns of behaviour from the other attendees, we tend to form our opinions and think the same way after a while. This is why going back into the real world after a spiritual retreat actually feels 'painful', as we are all again exposed to people who have not bonded over the experiences that we all have. This phenomenon of 'transference' can also be seen in a graduating class; a tight-knit forum or any such groups of which the individuals which have spent a considerable amount of time with each other. In fact, the implications behind this is very nicely articulated by an American rapper, Nipsey Hussle:

"If you look at the people in your circle and don't get inspired, then you don't have a circle. You have a cage."

So in the midst of any type of hardship - it would be wise to look out for people who can provide a sense of inspiration and strength. Also, because of the phenomenon of transference, being others whom we can learn from with is another way our brains can learn to adjust to adverse situations.

INSIGHT: What unique insights can this challenge provide us with?

"The obstacle is the path"
-Zen Proverb

Ironically, suffering and experiencing pain can also give us the impetus we need to find a better solution, (which we may have not have even considered before). Psychologist Gary Klein refers to this as "creative desperation"[59] . This was a term originally coined by Dutch psychologist Adrian de Groot, as he described the brilliant strategies chess players would come up with when backed into a corner.

> This phenomenon of creative desperation - as long as we are not stressed - helps us figure out new and better solutions to gain insight.

So what may appear as a limitation can actually act as a catalyst, which then forces us to devise better solutions to our problems. There are countless stories of people who have overcome hardships and even found their purpose in life through this concept of creative desperation.

SELF GROWTH: What can this situation teach me about myself that I wasn't consciously aware of before?

"She didn't struggle and so she didn't grow".
Paulo Coelho

Difficult times gift us the opportunity to explore our inner self. At times, it appears that the true obstacle isn't the obstacle in front of us, but instead the obstacle within ourselves. Perhaps it's our inflexibility, our arrogance, or our fear that causes us to remain still and unable to move forward. Not long ago, I found myself trapped in a reactive cycle of rumination because I was triggered by a close acquaintance. I found out that this lady had point-blank lied to my face about an important matter. Since it had been a long time since someone had had 'the nerve' to lie to me and get away with it, I didn't quite frankly know how to react. Did she think I would never find out? With a certain misaligned confidence, I reacted out of anger and picked up the phone to confront her.

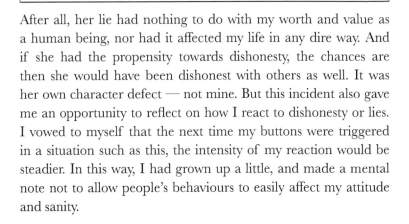

> **What I should have done was just not take it personally.**

After all, her lie had nothing to do with my worth and value as a human being, nor had it affected my life in any dire way. And if she had the propensity towards dishonesty, the chances are then she would have been dishonest with others as well. It was her own character defect — not mine. But this incident also gave me an opportunity to reflect on how I react to dishonesty or lies. I vowed to myself that the next time my buttons were triggered in a situation such as this, the intensity of my reaction would be steadier. In this way, I had grown up a little, and made a mental note not to allow people's behaviours to easily affect my attitude and sanity.

OPPORTUNITY: What doors can this challenging situation open up for me? And what doors can close to serve me better?

"Before something great happens, everything falls apart". Unknown

At times, challenging opportunities lead us to outcomes that are even better than what we had originally planned. For example, the women who had survived the horrific acid attacks, finally came to believe they could help others who had suffered through the same ordeal. They had a renewed sense of purpose in their lives again. How many inspirational stories are built on this concept? These dark moments of desperation can sometimes bring out the best in us. One of my favourite quotes that I keep laminated is, "Failure shows us the way — by showing us what isn't the way."[60]

SUMMARY

When 'bad' things happen in our life, we have a natural desire to fix or control the issue. If the circumstances don't allow for this, it is natural for us to ruminate or feel the injustice of it all. But again, this makes life even harder to deal with. The mental resistance to a challenge, problem or pain-point makes it an even bigger obstacle than the actual obstacle itself. Whenever you find yourself stuck, reflect on the VAISO formula.

- **What virtues can you practice and hone into?** For example, will this situation make you feel more gratitude for what you actually do have in life?
- **In what way can you adjust if you can't control the situation?** Would it be a good move to find people who can guide you in the right way or provide you with the right company?
- **What insight can you gain from this?** Is there a new path that has emerged which can benefit you in the future?
- **Can you see areas in which you are 'part of the problem'?** How does this problem contribute to your self-growth?
- **In what way has this issue enhanced your understanding of where you were headed and where you now want to go?** What opportunities does it present for you?

CHAPTER 9

ALTRUISM
THE POWER OF SERVICE

*"The day you feel hopeless and horrible, on that day get out of your room &
ask people: 'What can I do you for you?' That service will bring a revolution
inside you."*
Sri Sri Ravi Shankar

*Nice guys finish last? Certainly not! A whole plethora of research has come
together to confirm how helping others and engaging in selfless service is not
only an integral part of our bio-psychology, but also a huge benefactor for deep
fulfilment. But here again, we are put to the test. Are we motivated to serve
others only so we may gain respect or score brownie points with others? Or
are we motivated to help and be of service out of genuine compassion? This
chapter explores how as human beings, we are actually hardwired to 'give' and
serve others without the expectation of reward. It also explores how our good
health and wellbeing is correlated to the amount of service we do, and how to
find meaningful service in what we might think are the most trivial of things.*

On a humid Saturday afternoon, I was strolling through
Singapore's iconic and expansive Botanical Gardens, on my way
to pick up my daughter from a fishing playdate. Already late, I
weaved through the shrubbery, trying to catch a glimpse of that
evasive lake they were at. Realising I was actually lost amongst all
the green, I suddenly heard a soft whimper, "Mama, mama!"

As my heart skipped a beat, I hastened my step and peeked my head around a looming shrub. What appeared to be a young boy - perhaps around four years old − was seen nonchalantly gazing around, with one foot firmly on his scooter and the other on the gravel. He then turned around towards me, tears rolling down his face - and for a brief moment paused hopefully. But the biggest wave of disappointment cascaded his face as his eyes quietly accused,

"You are not my mother!"

Glumly, he jumped back onto his scooter and skated ahead. I instinctively followed his trail and meekly called out to him, "I'll help you find your mummy." He didn't turn back, and soon enough, I lost him in that green maze of twists and turns. My heart sank.

After catching sight of him again, I hesitantly followed him as he conducted his elusive search. Here I was a late and lost mother about to collect her daughter, chasing a little boy who had also ironically lost his own mother.

I quietly trailed behind his red t-shirt as he sped across the hill. A few minutes later, we both reached the Park Centre Meeting Point. Precipitously, he pointed and exclaimed in joy *"Mama!"* and sped towards a heavily pregnant woman who was kneeling down to tie her toddler's shoelace. She looked up and smiled casually at her son, perhaps oblivious of what he had just been through.

I quietly passed her in anger and headed towards the lakeside area. A huge part of me wanted to face the mother head-on and lecture her about how unsafe it was to leave a small child unattended in such a big park. But then another part of me also wanted to see how I would react to just keeping silent and moving on. Sometimes I like to test myself like that - if I am present enough to do so.

But that is also when I noticed a powerful internal shift take over.

Such a small act of service (even though the boy and mother were totally unaware) had left me feeling strangely satisfied. Why? Reflecting back, it is most likely because I had left my minor annoyances behind as my focus had shifted on helping the child.

But even more importantly - knowing I had done some 'good' and had acted out of pure compassion (with no obligation towards anyone), incited a warm fuzzy sensation within. *So this is what true altruism felt like* - I mused. Relieved and feeling a little more at peace, I finally caught sight of my jubilant daughter waving from across the lake, and ran towards her to give her a tight hug.

THE SCIENCE OF ALTRUISM: BORN TO BE GOOD

Altruistic behaviour is when we selflessly act to promote someone else's welfare, regardless of how it may affect us. Donald Pfaff, an acclaimed neuroscientist and author of *The Altruistic Brain* argues that we are "born to be good", that the human brain is "wired to propel us towards empathic behaviour and feelings leading to altruistic behaviors."[61] In fact, the act of understanding our naturally altruistic brain further enables us to perform even more benevolent actions characterised by - not just heroic actions - but simple everyday kindness. This view is in stark contrast to the older, popular views of Hobbes, Rousseau, etc., who claim that human beings are naturally self-serving and only act for the welfare of others under a social contract (such as the Law).

But what does Pfaff really mean by "born to be good"?

While proposing his *Altruistic Brain Theory*, he cites that, "a guiding principle of a healthy human brain is 'First act morally, then ask why."[62] It is clear from his research that our brains are naturally wired to empathise with other human beings; to be compassionate towards another; to be sensitive to others' emotions, and to care about others' well-being.

Although the majority of these altruistic tendencies may very well fall below our conscious radar, they are very much real and form a large part of the motivation towards our everyday actions.

It is no wonder that, at times, we experience something known as vicarious or 'second-hand embarrassment' when watching someone making a blunder out of themselves (especially in public situations). While I write this, my mind takes me back to a recent conference I had attended. As the event was coming to a close, the last invited guest speaker started walking towards the stage. With his head and eyes faced down, he slowly waddled himself up onto the stage and after what seemed like a really long time, he finally looked up at the expectant audience. Grabbing the microphone nervously, he opened his mouth to speak while looking out at all of us - and nothing came out except a muffled cough. Feeling utmost embarrassment for the speaker, I also could feel the tension of the room building up. As I looked around me, I noticed some of the participants keenly leaning forward as if to encourage him to keep going. Someone was gripping their hands looking around and I noticed a few people looking down to avoid his gaze. After a few attempts and some feeble coughs, still no words could come out. Perhaps at that point, he realised there was no point going on. He looked down ashamed and stumbled quickly off the stage. Feeling a wave of deep compassion for him, I realised how through watching him in that awkward position on stage, it could have very easily been me in that situation. It is obvious from the audience's reaction that they would have felt the same way too.

Many studies demonstrate that this type of natural behaviour - vicarious embarrassment- is induced by our human sense of empathy.

And this, in fact, happens regardless of whether we have any connection with the other person's situation. In fact, a recent report provides neurological evidence of this phenomenon as it showed that "the anterior cingulate cortex and the left anterior insula, two cortical structures typically involved in vicarious feelings of others' pain, are strongly implicated in experiencing the 'social pain' for others' flaws and pratfalls".[63]

As I skimmed through this research, I realised how intuitively true this was.

Most of us would instinctively cringe if we were to see a nervous performer suddenly stumbling on stage. And we might even automatically reach out to help somebody who looks like they are about to trip. Children have this natural inclination to resonate with others' joys and sadness too. In fact, both of my children flush with embarrassment when a stranger belches unabashedly in a restaurant. Why? Because as human beings, our natural instinct is to reach out and help others so *they* can avoid experiencing pain. This is largely because our brains associate ourselves to be in the exact same position as the other who is actually experiencing the pain. This empathetic instinct is, in my opinion, a miraculous phenomenon and quite possibly a determining factor for what bonds each of us to one another and also keep the ties of humanity strong.

So, since the research shows that we are hardwired for altruism and are naturally built to resonate with other people's joy and sadness - how is this actually reflected in our brain?

This phenomenon is explained through the function of mirror neurons. A mirror neuron is a type of neuron in our brain that 'mirrors' or simulates the action of another, as though we ourselves are performing the action. This explains why when one person sighs, it triggers a chain reaction of sighs in a group. You will also notice the same thing occurring when one person in a group yawns, the others are prompted to yawn as well.

> The neuron "mirrors" the behaviour of the other, as though the observer were itself acting. ❧

If, for example, a stranger suddenly smiles at you, notice your tendency to automatically smile back without the need to really understand what the other person's intention is.

A number of cognitive psychologists believe that these mirror neurons are responsible for feelings of empathy. Dr. Marco Iacoboni, a neuroscientist that studies the phenomenon, writes in the *New York Times:*

"When you see me pull my arm back, as if to throw the ball, you also have in your brain a copy of what I am doing and it helps you understand my goal. Because of mirror neurons, you can read my intentions. You know what I am going to do next…And if you see me choke up, in emotional distress…, mirror neurons in your brain simulate my distress. You automatically have empathy for me. You know how I feel because you literally feel what I am feeling."[64]

It is no wonder then, that when tears well up in your eyes, the person you're with might also have the same impulse to tear up too. It is these types of phenomena that trigger our altruistic tendencies. But from an evolutionary perspective, were we always naturally altruistic?

IT'S IN OUR DNA: ALTRUISM FROM AN EVOLUTIONARY PERSPECTIVE

In today's self-oriented and social media savvy world, it is sometimes unimaginable to believe that we are hardwired to be altruistic. Hence, it is stirring to understand how human beings evolved this altruistic behaviour and why it plays such a vital role in our everyday behaviours.

Pfaff proposes that altruism most likely evolved to allow early humans to expand their lineage and survive in a hostile environment. He suggests that the drive to have sex and child rearing could have guided humans to expand their altruistic tendencies with the goal to include more people into their tribe.

Experiments have been done to show that altruism actually begins as early as 18 months old. A team of psychologists, from *Max Planck Institute for Evolutionary Anthropology* in Germany, measured the sympathetic arousal of 56 toddlers as they witnessed particular situations where an adult did not receive help. Through studying the physiology and instinctive interactions of the children, the results demonstrated that even very young children have a natural tendency to help other persons solve their problems. They observe, "We found that the motivation for young children's helping behaviour is simply that the person in need should be helped. Young children's early helping," they write, "is motivated by a genuine concern for the welfare of the person in need."[65] It is hence clear that the impulse to help without any expectation of reward is hardwired into our biology from a young age.

Increasing Our Health & Happiness Quotient

Numerous studies have been piloted on adults which illustrate that any act of altruism increases our 'happiness quotient'. A team from *Harvard Business School* conducted a series of experiments that gave subjects the choice of spending money either on themselves or on others. They found that participants who spent money, even as little as $5, on someone else experienced much greater happiness than those who spent it on themselves.[66]. This study also implies that:

> Giving a gift will make the brain just as happy, if not more, as receiving it.

Allan Luks, author of *The Healing Power of Doing Good*, surveyed approximately 3000 volunteers and found that those who helped regularly were ten times more likely to be in good health than those who didn't.

Luks proposes that there may be a biochemical explanation behind this, known as the "helpers high". When we experience this phenomenon, a steady stream of endorphins gets released into our bloodstream - thereby reducing any pain or stress we might have been previously experiencing. Not only this, it also helps induce feelings of euphoria and general well-being. In fact, those who volunteered regularly reported "sensations of warmth and greater energy".[67]

Remember that warm and fuzzy feeling I felt after the little boy found his mother in the park? Stephen G. Post, Director of the *Center for Medical Humanities, Compassionate Care and Bioethics* in New York, labels this warmth or euphoria as the "giver's glow". He explains that the response is triggered by a biochemical reaction in the part of brain which actually recognises rewarding stimuli: "Philanthropy doles out several different happiness chemicals including dopamine, endorphins that give people a sense of euphoria and oxytocin, which is associated with tranquillity, serenity or inner peace."[68]

We are designed to be kind. In fact, psychiatrist Alberto Alberti says that "Love not expressed becomes hate, joy not being enjoyed becomes depression."

So the next time you feel hesitant or shy to help the blind man up the escalator or the pregnant mother get off the bus, remember that you are born with this instinct and only stand to benefit by extending your service.

LIVE YOUR LIFE WITH MEANING: IT BEGINS WITH THE SMALL THINGS

Donating to charity or volunteering are not the only ways to help people.

> If one were to really seek out - our world is full of opportunities to make someone feel good.

A warm smile at the boy sitting on his own in the school canteen; an effort to give the right change to the old taxi driver; curiosity about the stewardess's next stopover; a 'thank you for everything you do' message to your personal assistant; or even a simple compliment to the chef who tirelessly created a dish, are only just a few small examples of actions that can add to an altruistic life.

Even contributing for the 'greater good', such as taking care of the environment in some way, is also a fundamental part of altruism. Such examples could be something as simple as disposing an empty can from the street; taking part in a beach clean-up; picking up a stray cat and helping it find shelter; calling a dangerous pothole to the attention to the authorities, and of course much more. Being aware of these small yet powerful actions, will in natural course, prime your brain to identify more over time. In fact, you will soon see opportunities start to crop up everywhere and this altruistic tendency will eventually become a large part of who you are.

I experienced this wonderful phenomenon a few years ago. At the start of a silent yoga retreat, we were divided into teams for the purpose of giving back to the community. Every day, we were to devote two hours performing volunteer work at the resort where we stayed. Day one comprised of raking the leaves from the resort grounds. On day two, we served food to our group and would proceed to eat last. On day three, we were to take turns washing the dishes and keeping them away. And this would go on for another 3 days with other such similar service-based activities. We were instructed to do this in small and efficient groups with silent communication and minimal eye contact.

On Day 1, I found myself struggling. In an unusually sceptical frame of mind, I was mulling over questions such as: 'How does raking leaves correlate with my spiritual growth? How does this help other people feel good? And more importantly, 'Why is everyone passive-aggressively competing for the 1 garden rake?' Rest assured and watching everyone's faces - I was pretty sure I was not alone in these thoughts. I watched in amusement as the silent charade of winning the longest rake began.

On Day 2, I noticed a little shift. It could have been that we were all settling into the routine better, but I did observe that everyone including myself seemed to be more peaceful - more in the flow of 'service'. As I washed the dishes, I felt a little more in resonance with the group as we handed over one plate to another in silence.

By Day 3, things were visibly starting to change. Instead of battling over who could get the longest rake, teammates started handing them over to one another. People started to spend longer in the kitchen cleaning up and as a result, postponed their desire to eat. If an outsider were to walk into the resort, they would have seen groups dressed in white working together in a cohesive and concentrated silence.

On Day 4, the difference in all of us was palpable. Two things happened. I, myself, felt a sort of profound freedom. The acts of service actually distracted me away from my constant internal rationalising. Secondly, a strong sensation of unconditional compassion took over. Rather than thinking of my own needs, I genuinely wanted the resort guests to experience a clean and healthy environment. I genuinely wanted the meals to be served to others nice and hot. I genuinely wanted the tired resort staff to sit down and relax while we helped stack up the dishes. The true act of '*seva*' (service) was taking over. In just days, it was clear that being in service to others was becoming a part of my new nature.

Finally, when the retreat headed into its last day and it was time to say our goodbyes, something extraordinary lingered in all of us. We had learned a gift. Besides learning what it really took to go out and help others with no conditions attached, we realised it did not leave us feeling empty or running after approval. Instead paradoxically, it left us feeling more fulfilled. Upon reflection with one another, we spoke about how we were all overcome with a need to keep our hands busy in service.

Rather than the recognition which may or may not come with 'giving back', the real sense of wholeness and freedom only occurs when our offer of service flows naturally and unconditionally.

While following the little boy in the park, I could hear myself scolding the mother in my mind, "How can you leave such a small boy around the park to roam unattended?" But also lurking behind that internal dialogue was the self-righteous voice of someone who wanted to be recognised as a saviour, a heroine. This kind of recognition is meaningless, temporary and unfulfilling. Strengthening the ego with small acts of recognition is practically akin to indulging into a piece of candy. In no time, the high would be gone and we'd be craving another!

> Instead, working quietly to help others actually leads us to a powerful place of fulfilment.

No-one says it better than Pier Ferrucci in his book *The Power of Kindness*: "If our true goal is to gain admiration and recognition, show how good we are, or collect brownie points, sooner or later we will give up. If instead the motivation is to help someone heal, feel better, find herself, know what to do and make progress in her growth, then we will continue. Service helps us purify our motivation, become disinterested, and therefore freer."[69]

Craving admiration and recognition traps us further within our egoistic tendencies, causing an addictive cycle of praise and reward. This can be detrimental to our mental health when we do not get the recognition we think we deserve. Indeed, what we can learn is that there is a certain type of freedom in not having to prove ourselves to others. Of course, the other problem with a need for recognition is that we tend to get lost in other people's demands and expectations. As a result of this, we lose out on the real experience of our instinctive and compassionate nature.

Since re-aligning ourselves with this 'giving reflex' is such an integral part of our own and other's well-being, there are many ways to help others on how to tap into their altruistic natures.

Support Your Kids without Excessive Praise. If you are a parent, you will know that the reward system is still highly prevalent in academic institutions and society. But one path-breaking study showed that children who received material rewards for helping others eventually became *less likely* to help in the future, unlike those who only receive verbal praise or received no reward at all.[70] This study verifies that external rewards tend to undermine children's natural altruistic instinct. As we have seen from the research above, even the youngest children are intrinsically motivated to be kind. So extrinsic rewards can undermine this tendency.

Modelling to Influence Others. Another technique to promote altruism at home is through modelling altruistic behaviour, because people watching you engage in giving behaviour will also tend to emulate your actions. In fact, in a study conducted by James Fowler and Nicholas Christakis, also authors of "Connected: The Surprising Power of Our Social Networks", it was found that witnessing altruistic behaviour creates a cascading effect in social circles. This means that it actually promoted altruistic actions in social circles that were not even part of the original interaction, and spread up to three degrees of separation (from person to person to person to person).[71]

One of the reasons this phenomenon spreads is because of 'elevation'.

This term has been defined by psychologists as the feeling we get when we see unexpected acts of goodness. It's like that feeling you get when you see a young man going out of his way to help an elderly person cross the road.

In this case, you might describe yourself experiencing a 'touching' or 'heart-warming' emotion. That is a clear example of the phenomenon of 'elevation', and as a result of this, it is possible you will feel more inspired than you usually would, to undertake other forms of altruistic action.

THOUGHTS ON GIVING

Having delved into the academic research behind the notion of altruism, I now leave you with some profound realisations by the greatest thinkers of our time:

> "Before giving, the mind of the giver is happy; while giving, the mind of the giver is made peaceful; and having given, the mind of the giver is uplifted."
>
> *- Lord Buddha*

> "The heart that gives, gathers."
>
> *- Tao Te Cheng*

> "For it is in giving that we receive."
>
> *- Saint Francis of Assisi*

> "We rise by lifting others."
>
> *- Robert Ingersoll*

> "The best way to find yourself is to lose yourself in the service of others."
>
> *- Mahatma Gandhi*

> "Only a life lived for others is a life worthwhile."
>
> *- Albert Einstein*

> "Life's most persistent and urgent question, 'What are you doing for others?'"
>
> *- Martin Luther King Jr.*

SUMMARY

Not only does the science confirm that our compassionate instinct is an integral part of human behaviour, but being of service towards others has many profound benefits for our well-being, health and longevity.

We have learned that:

- Altruistic behaviours are hardwired into our biology as **young children**, even as young as 18 months old.
- Being altruistically natured allowed early humans to **expand their lineage and survive** in a hostile environment.
- **Giving** a gift will make the brain just as happy, if not more so, as receiving it.
- Those who helped regularly were **10 times more likely to be in good health** than those who didn't.
- A phenomenon known as **'givers glow'** (endorphins being released into the bloodstream) is known to reduce pain or stress and instead induce feelings of euphoria and general well-being.

We can promote such altruistic behaviour by being wary of the reward system for our children; model this behaviour to incite elevation in others; and educate others and spread the message on how our brain is wired for goodwill.

Chapter 10

Courage
The Success Paradigm

"Our deepest fear is not that we are inadequate. Our deepest fear is that we are powerful beyond measure. It is our light, not our darkness that most frightens us. We ask ourselves, who am I to be brilliant, gorgeous, talented, fabulous? Actually, who are you not to be? You are a child of God. Your playing small does not serve the world. There is nothing enlightened about shrinking so that other people won't feel insecure around you. We are all meant to shine, as children do. We were born to make manifest the glory of God that is within us. It's not just in some of us; it's in everyone. And as we let our own light shine, we unconsciously give other people permission to do the same. As we are liberated from our own fear, our presence automatically liberates others."

Marianne Williamson, *A Return to Love*

For most of us, the fear of failing ignites uncomfortable emotions within. But could there possibly be a level of fear - much deeper and much more complex - that is preventing us from reaching our utmost potential? In this chapter, we discuss one of the most unrecognised and underrated fears - the fear of success, also known as achievemephobia. Although we can certainly understand why one wants to avoid failure, how is it possible that one may not want to succeed? Is it possible that we can even learn to fear our own power? Here, we look closely at how tangible this fear can exist in our lives, and explore some common triggers and limiting beliefs which contribute to this phenomenon.

Since humans covet the term 'success' so much in our lives, it might seem counter intuitive that one would actually want to turn away from it - especially when it is just within grasp.

If you have ever experienced this phenomenon, perhaps you might have gone through situations such as:

You have been working for months to reach your goal weight and then catch yourself progressively cheating.

You procrastinate working on projects that could lead to recognition because you feel you are not worthy.

You think to yourself "this is too good to last" whenever you experience a sense of achievement or a successful outcome.

At times, these internal beliefs bypass our consciousness so quickly, we might even miss it. In fact, if we are so used to this internal dialogue running through our daily reel, we might only catch them out when we read it somewhere or hear someone else point it out to us. But for some of us they are very much real and pervasive - dictating how we live our lives, the risks we take, and our general enjoyment factors.

By the same token, I have never heard any of my clients say to me, "I do *not* want to achieve great things in my life." On the contrary, most sessions are usually discourses based around their everyday fears such as: the fear of choosing the wrong career; the fear of embarrassing themselves in front of others; the fear of their husband cheating; the fear of their kids failing at school; the fear of saying the wrong thing, the fear of in-laws; the fear of them not finding their passion and so on.

So, this begs the question:

Why is the fear of success so elusive and hard to spot within ourselves?

Here are three possible explanations, which we will explore in more detail later.

- The fear of success is deeply engrained into our belief systems from very early on in our lives. What is interesting is that these belief systems underlying the fear of achievement are fundamentally unconscious in nature and might be easy to miss if we do not recognise the signs.

- The fear of success could be silently masquerading itself as the fear of failure, and one would not know the difference. (We will explore the difference later.)

- It is not the pinnacle of success itself that is the problem but rather the fear of the side effects that come with being successful in our endeavours, many of which may be genuinely undesirable. (For example, the side effect of becoming a successful and popular reality TV star would be the media not giving you the integrity of space or privacy.)

Although the idea of achievemephobia might seem fairly new to some, this phenomenon has been researched with strong interest over decades. In fact, Abraham Maslow was one of the first humanistic psychologists to point out and explain it in a metaphorical context. He categorically named this phenomenon '*The Jonah Complex*', after the biblical story of Jonah - a prophet who attempted to 'run away from his fate and hide from God'.

The story went like this. A devoted man to the laws of God, Jonah was much looked up to and revered by the people of Israel. One day, God requested Jonah whom he believed to be the best person for the task, to go and reprimand their arch-enemy neighbouring city, Nineveh. So, Jonah was to request the disobeying people of Irvine to follow the laws of God and stay away from evil. But, Jonah, out of fear, decided not to follow His God's orders and actually escaped on a ship to another country. The story then goes on to show how His God was not happy with this and punished him with a storm at sea.

Abraham Maslow drew parallels to this story by relating it to the humanistic fear of success.

He explains that so often we run away from our responsibilities of 'nature', or our inner potential and abilities - just as Jonah tried in vain to run away from his fate.

Maslow believed that, "It is certainly possible for most of us to be greater than we are in actuality. We all have unused potentials or not fully developed ones...So often we run away from the responsibilities dictated (or rather suggested) by nature, by fate, even sometimes by accident, just as Jonah tried—in vain—to run away from his fate...We are generally afraid to become that which we can glimpse in our most perfect moments, under the most perfect conditions, under conditions of greatest courage."[72]

ANXIETY & PHOBIAS: ACHIEVEMEPHOBIA

Since then, however, most scientists and psychologists agree that this humanistic fear of success exists for both men and women. So real is this fear that it has been termed achievemephobia. A writer on Anxiety and Phobias, Jacob Oleson writes, "While many phobias can be hidden from public display, like the phobia of failure, it is impossible to cover up achievemephobia...The fear of success controls cognitive processing in direct proportion to the significance of the issue confronted. The more significant the success to the person's way of life, the more likely he will freeze up."[73]

Thankfully, there are a number of processes out there to identify and to help overcome this phenomenon of 'achievemephobia'.

For example, in the field of Neuro-Linguistic Programming, there is a popular cognitive process to help us deal with internal conflict, known as The Parts Integration. As human beings, we naturally have parts of us which cannot decide which path to take - so we are held back, confused and make excuses for not carrying out important tasks. Of course this creates an unpleasant conflict within us. For example, while we may be thrilled to receive an A+ on an entrance exam, there might be a part of us that is averse to getting a high grade. Why? Perhaps we are intimidated at the thought of being accepted into a school far away from home. Or perhaps we are averse to the idea of being pulled into a prestigious institution as it might alienate us from our friends. The Parts Integration process aims to unite the craving and the aversion so that one feels metaphorically whole once again and can realign with ones' values quickly.

WHY WE NEED TO REDEFINE SUCCESS IN OUR BRAINS

> **Success is actually a highly convoluted concept. The very word itself represents a 'come and go' phenomenon – somewhat temporary and fleeting.**

And one of the biggest misconceptions of our era comes from how we interpret and imagine real success to be. Our collective idea of success centres on getting ahead of others: more money, more fame, more visibility, and hence more power over others.

But, as we know, the irony with success is that one day you can be riding high on the Stock Exchange and the next - down in the deep pits of debt hell. But what if the concept of 'success' could be reframed in our minds as reaching towards what gives us self-actualisation?

Reaching a state of self-actualisation is much more potent for us than winning a lottery or clinching a deal, because real personal satisfaction occurs when we are able to use our given talents and innate creativities. When we are able to tap into this, a very prominent curtain (which shields us from the rest of the world), is metaphorically lifted and we are able to experience true expression.

> With true expression, comes a sense of freedom and aliveness.
>
> ⤷

As if this were not enough, when we delve into what we love doing most, the joy of 'doing' increases and success inevitably becomes a by-product.

Also, when we tap into our store-well of talents, creativities and passions - we are able to also tap into something even more important - and that is self-love. Simply put, when we do things that we love or have a talent for, we are nurturing ourselves and creating a steady sense of personal well-being.

Abraham Maslow, who is most famous for his term 'self-actualisation' described the term as a desire "to become everything one is capable of becoming."[74] The meaning of the term is clear and on point - that reaching one's own highest potential should reward one with a sense of internally recognised success.

> The key here is - not success to society but as per ourselves.
>
> ⤷

As Maslow fervently pointed out, all human beings follow their own path. For example, the way you see your own growth and capabilities can be totally different from how your child views his own. So achieving self-actualisation is not a typical run of the mill process, and can be very different from one person to the next. This raises the question, what does self-actualization really look like? When first describing self-actualization, Maslow remarked that: "[a] musician must make music, an artist must paint, a poet must write, if he is to be ultimately happy. What a man can be, he must be."[75]

For this very reason, the way we view success is critical to how we work towards our goals. It holds much more weight than just achieving fame or credibility, but in fact more about working actively towards self-actualisation.

Stuck on the same tedious goal for years? The painful truth is - if your goals drag on or are stuck in the same continuum for a long time - it is possible that on a profound level, there is a part of you which does *not* actually want it. And because tracing what holds us back is crucial to us moving forward, we really do owe it to ourselves to investigate whether this is the case or not (especially if the goal is robbing us of valuable time). One powerful and quick way to do this is to delve into whether our fear of success shows up in particular behaviours. Here are some tell-tale signs:

Procrastination

As mentioned earlier, it may not be the success we fear, but its side consequences. For example, a college applicant might experience some anxiety about the 'hard work' that comes as a by-product of getting accepted into a prestigious university. Or a successful job applicant may fear the thought of making new friends and colleagues at a new job. As a result of these fears, people tend to procrastinate to avoid the inevitable.

> "Procrastination is the fear of success. People procrastinate because they are afraid of the success that they know will result if they move ahead now. Because success is heavy, carries a responsibility with it, it's easier to procrastinate and live on the "someday I'll" philosophy."
>
> – Denis Waitley

No Clear Calling

Almost all adults (at least by their late twenties or early thirties) would have an inkling for what it is they would like to do in their lives. But if we are not consciously aware of what passions and talents tug at our hearts, it is possibly because we do not believe we have the 'potential' to do something great. One might even think the whole concept of 'true calling' or having a 'passion' as just hocus-pocus and created to make people feel good about themselves. Instead, one may even feel it is safer to follow the crowd, follow the trends and do what everyone else is doing. It might feel better to them to stay within their comfort zone, of which they experience no criticism or judgement. This is a sure-shot sign that a person has been running away from 'themselves' for some time, (the possible reasons for which we will look into later.)

Anxiety

It is very common that people who have experienced traumatic events in their lives are actually gripped by fear just as they are about to achieve a successful outcome. Psychotherapist Susanne Babbel writes, "I've had first-hand experience coaching clients whose past experience feeds their current fear of success. For them, the excitement of success feels uncomfortably close to the feeling of arousal they experienced when subjected to a traumatic event or multiple events. People who have experienced trauma may associate the excitement of success with the same physiological reactions as trauma. They avoid subjecting themselves to excitement-inducing circumstances, which causes them to be almost phobic about success."[76]

Aversion to the Spotlight

As a general personality trait, you might find yourself often retreating from being the centre of attention and staying well within the shadows. Introvert people in particular dislike being caught in the spotlight, which is why success can seem so unattractive to them.

SO, WHY ARE WE AFRAID OF BEING BRILLIANT?

Just like two sides of a coin - both the fear of failure and the fear of success - play a central mantle in how we approach our lives. They are both an indication to how we treat ourselves; how worthy we feel internally; how much we think we deserve to be happy; and of how we can make an impact once we realise our potential.

One of my most loyal clients was most adamant about her 'inability' to stick to a diet and had a fixed viewpoint that all diets didn't work on her and were deemed therefore as 'a waste of time'. After years of trying, she just could not lose weight to reach her desired goal. She would come in and attest to her 'failures'; her little midnight cheats; her arguments with her nutritionist; and stories of how she succumbed constantly to temptation. For months I would feel dismayed when she would come back dejected and still extremely overweight. After careful analysis, together we used an NLP process to dig deeper into her psyche and came to realise it was a lot more than the 'small' mistakes she was constantly making. It was actually her fear of becoming thin that was ultimately holding her back. Is that really possible? Very much so.

As we gently sifted through her history, (with the use of mild hypnotherapy,) we were able to trace all the way back to the triggers which were causing her everyday eating habits. We explored her core belief system which lead us to see what she truly thought of herself and of her life. We learned that extra padding on her meant "she felt safe", and also to her surprise that "she would not fall ill" if she was on the heavier side. She discovered, this was because as a very young child she watched, frightened, as her grandmother's health started to deteriorate and noticed her body shrink drastically the same time. Being young and naïve, after a while a core belief was formed. Eventually, being skinny metaphorically equated to 'illness' and 'disease' to her. So because of this survival-based core belief, throughout her life she would resist losing weight thinking it was the 'healthy' thing to do. To make matters worse - whenever she would fall ill - her mother would innocently tell her she was sick because she was not eating enough.

So, tracing back to the triggers of these fears are actually fundamental to finding a current day solution. In this sense, we need to find out what triggers cause us to become fearful of achieving a successful outcome in the first place.

Self Esteem & Core Beliefs.

> By design, core beliefs are our very own personal blueprint of instructions that determine the values, ideas and actions in our lives.

Our beliefs are concepts that we believe to be true about life and ourselves. For instance, if a person says that he is outgoing we can assume that he has the belief "I am outgoing" stored somewhere in his memory bank - his subconscious mind. This will ultimately lead him to behave in an outgoing and maybe even a friendly manner.

The belief systems we hold serve as an attitude or as a "lens" through which we perceive the outside world. There are beliefs that empower us, and there are those that don't. These are also known as 'limiting beliefs'. Metaphorically speaking, beliefs are the stories we tell ourselves about what we can and cannot do in life.

These powerful beliefs are sometimes not easily accessible or visible, because they are held in the subconscious mind just outside the realm of conscious awareness. They are hard to grasp onto, because they go unquestioned for so long and most of the time. In fact, because we cannot hear them, touch them or see them, we are not even conscious that these beliefs are running in the background reel of our lives. As a result, we may not understand why and how we overreacted to a situation, got overly upset at someone, or even cried during a non-emotional scene in a movie.

As Carl Jung rightly said:

"Until you make the unconscious conscious, it will direct your life and you will call it fate."

At a point when limiting beliefs start hampering your progress and self-expression or causing you harm, it would benefit you to start considering where, how and why these beliefs originated.

TYPICAL 'LIMITING BELIEF' STATEMENTS

We had earlier touched on how limiting beliefs can silently dictate how we 'live' our lives, but that also at times they are also elusive to get hold of.

Do you hear yourself in some of these statements? Here are some common and core negative limiting beliefs that can block people from attaining self-actualization:

"The more successful I become, the more people will need me. I am scared because I do not want to let them down."

The responsibility (side-effect) of being accountable to more people due to a sudden increase in popularity, a promotion or a succession might scare one into believing they are not capable of living up to other's expectations. Hence, the avoidance pattern sets in and one would rather fail, than achieve, and risk letting others down.

"I am not capable without the help of…"

I once had a fairly elderly client who had recognised that she was hoisting a deep psychological block. The problem was that her whole life, she constantly felt like she could not achieve anything worthwhile without some form of external support. As we delved deeper, we discovered that her negative self-talk led her to believe, at a young age, that she was simply not capable of doing things independently. As she narrated, phrases such as "you cannot do this alone" or "do not get too ahead of yourself" was common talk in her household. Thus, most of her accomplishments were always linked to the limiting belief that she could not be successful without her parents' or others' backing. This eventually extended to her being heavily dependent on not only her parents - but her spouse, her children, and her friends. So, her whole life she felt like everything that she did, which was good and worthy, was attributed to the support of the people closest to her. And if for some reason, anyone disapproved of her behaviour or actions, she would be disturbed for days. The problem with this internalised negative feedback is that, a child who has always heard comments like "you will not succeed without my help" possibly might just carry that belief well into adulthood. This can cause them to second guess and doubt every action that they take, and hence further lower their self-esteem while they rely on others for assistance.

It is the very same way we might have been taught by our elders or teachers to be suspicious of 'too many good things', and that 'good times never last'. This is where the 'too good to be true' mind-set comes from and one can either choose to believe it or live in the present moment.

"I was just lucky."

At what point does one start to believe that they are actually capable of achieving due to their current skills and capabilities, and not just as a stroke of luck or timing? A very real condition known as the "Impostor Syndrome"[77] has been labelled by psychologists where you believe your own success to be 'a charade on your own part', despite an undeniable track record of success. (The term was coined in 1978 by clinical psychologists Pauline R. Clance and Suzanne A. Imes.) Those living by this belief system remain convinced that they are 'frauds' and do not deserve the success they have achieved.

> How many times do you achieve something and turn around and credit it to just plain luck?

Studies have found that the impostor syndrome is particularly common amongst high-achievers. As a result of this, to avoid any successful outcome - people who carry this syndrome around with them keep themselves limited to a pattern of safe, low-profile, unchallenging and hence, uninteresting work.

"Change is scary."

It is normal to feel a certain amount of trepidation while entering uncharted territory or stepping out of one's comfort zone. In a new situation, one can potentially become afraid of being exposed to criticism, higher expectations, a new image or new pressures - despite the excitement or the hint of success offers. But if the concept of change is so threatening that it blocks you from reaching your potential - it would definitely help if you re-examine your belief system a little more.

Maybe as a child making decisions, you were taught to believe that it's better to be "safe than sorry".

Or while engaging with friends you were led to believe "better the devil you know than the one you don't know". Going through these limiting beliefs with a qualified psychotherapist or Life Coach (who can help you reprogram your way of thinking), can literally clear a new path for you to help you embrace change and a sense of renewal into your life.

"I don't know who I'll become."

The fear of turning into someone else who you don't like, (if you become successful), can severely hinder your goals. This fear has some foundation in reality. Imagine you are 40 kilos lighter just like you were during your bachelor days and had a whole line of women after you. You were officially dubbed the *"player"* and were not the most committed or faithful partner at the time. But, now that you are married with 3 kids and a loving wife - the thought of losing weight, becoming more attractive to women and possibly retreating into that bachelor mode might be tempting and hence scary. Therefore you put off exercising or dieting because of the fear of becoming 'the old you' who would put your family at risk. As baseless as it might seem, these are reasonable fears that people have.

"Others will reject me if I am successful."

Because of a deep psychological desire to belong to a social group or community, some of us would rather merge our beliefs with society and in the process - lose our individuality. The *Tall Poppy* syndrome describes certain features of society where people of high status are resented and criticised because they are technically now superior to the rest of the group.

> On some level, we have an innate fear that people will pull us back 'down to earth' if we succeed and rise above them.

This is similar to a phenomenon known as the 'crab mentality'. Whenever a crab in a bucket full of other crabs tries to get out, the others will pull it down as soon as it gets close to escaping. As a result of this psychological phenomenon, we allow ourselves to merge and conform to the rest of society's norms and end up ignoring our own goals and passions for fear of rejection.[78]

BREAKING UP WITH THE FEAR: IF NOT YOU, THEN WHO?

If you find yourself stuck and not sure what factors could be blocking your progress - here are some really effective ways to shift your perspective and get right down to your core triggers.

The Process of Chunking Down

If the offers are not coming in or the dollars are dwindling (despite sturdy efforts) it would be wise to identify the real problem area in your life. Now, you can start a process of chunking down your core beliefs, by asking yourself these questions and perhaps even writing the answers down:

What do you believe to be true about yourself or your life in order for this pattern to exist?

Has anyone ever said anything to you in your past which could have influenced your decisions today about this particular area?

What do I believe about achieving my desired goal or dream?

What scares me from achieving (my desired goal or dream? (i.e. the side-effects.)

Sometimes, a conversation with a specialist might give you a desired perspective for your problems. An NLP specialist will most likely use a technique known as time-line therapy to help you trace back to an unspecified time in the past when the belief first originated in your mind. They might also help you investigate what your 'secondary gain' is by not achieving a successful outcome. A very powerful technique would also be the Parts Integration Technique, (as discussed above), which would allow you to assess the different parts to your motivations and fears. If you cannot engage a Coach, even answering these questions down in a journal can surprise you into discovering a whole new dimension about yourself.

Learn How to Temporarily 'Step Out of Yourself'

Sometimes the idea of achievement and success needs to move beyond the "I". Often most of us humans are egocentric in nature and aim to please ourselves by achieving goals that have no real effect or impact on others' well-being. But the truth is, motivation that comes from helping others causes us to forget our fears even for a short while and, as a result, we are drawn into a world that is much larger than ourselves. So, it would be wise in this case to look beyond the "I" part of the goal, and seek to find a cause greater than our own self. In fact, we only stand to gain in perspective and compassion after considering what pain others are experiencing.

Rewind Back to Your 'Why'

Go back to why you wanted this goal in the first place. What is the best outcome that could come out of you achieving this?

> What motivated you to "press play" and set out on this journey?

Take maybe 15 minutes just to think about how your life will really change once you achieve your goal or pursued your passion. If you are at the tail end of editing your book, visualise yourself at the launch, signing copies after copies. If you are training for the marathon, imagine yourself finally crossing the final line. Or if you have been working on your political campaign, picture yourself walking on stage to a thundering applause. And then make an effort to really 'feel' how it feels when you have achieved this. This will remind you of why you even began in the first place.

Observe Your Patterns of Self-Sabotage as A Clue

You owe it to yourself to start documenting when, how and where the pattern of self-sabotage began.

> The self-sabotage we inflict upon ourselves is a great reminder to how our triggers can get the better of us.

At times, we forget that we do have the control to kick those patterns right out!

This means you might need to make visible changes around you, perhaps even by cleaning up your physical and mental environment. This could mean throwing away the potato chips; putting your phone into airplane mode; replacing your cigarettes with chewing gum or perhaps even distancing yourself from the friend who brings up toxic emotions within you.

Remind yourself that you have every right to enjoy the fruits of your gifts and talents, and in fact, not fulfilling your creative potential would possibly be doing a disservice to your fellow human beings. As Marianne Williamson very aptly says: "You are a child of God. Your playing small does not serve the world."

- **It's a very real phenomenon:** The fear of success (also known as 'achievemephobia') is a phenomenon that is much under discussed and unexplored - and yet it is responsible for so much of our misery. Unlike other phobias, which are widely discussed, we sometimes overlook what causes our very own fear of self-expression and self-actualisation. Not only do we block our creative potential, but we also wrongly end up berating ourselves, blaming our inability and lack of discipline for not achieving things.

- **The Side Effects of Success:** So, what causes us to sometimes avoid "success" in our lives? One such explanation is we have a fear of the side-effects that come with it. An example would be getting that much awaited promotion, which comes with the tag of more money and prestige. But the side effect could be having to live up to that new role, which will entail longer work hours and more work pressure.

- **Negative Limiting Beliefs:** From childhood, we could have been subjected to a number of limiting beliefs that have become so engrained in our psyche that they form part of our core belief systems. Some examples would be: "The more successful I become, the more people will need me and I do not want to let them down", and "I am not capable without the help of…"

Tips to break the block:

- **Chunking Down**. Asking the questions in the above chapter can help address the limiting beliefs that might have been hindering you all along, as well as sussing out the 'secondary gains' you unconsciously seek.

- **Practice Stepping Out of Yourself.** For greater motivation, look beyond the "I" part of the problem and seek to find a cause greater than yourself.

- **Rewind.** What motivated you to 'press play' and begin this journey?

- **Observe Your Patterns of Self-Sabotage as A Clue.** This means you to might need to make changes or clean up your physical and mental environment.

CHAPTER 11

FORGIVENESS
THE HIGHER ROAD. THE ONLY ROAD.

He who cannot forgive others
breaks the bridge over which he himself must pass.

Confucius

Dr Fred Luskin, Director of the Stanford University Forgiveness Project writes, "When your thoughts are full of bitterness, fear, self-pity and dreams of revenge, there is little room for love or for the quiet voice of guidance within you."[79] Ironically, although forgiveness is a well-known concept to us all, we sometimes misunderstand the act of forgiving others as a sign of weakness. On top of this, forgiving others is often arduous to practice, and it is especially difficult to forgive than to ask for forgiveness. At times, we are so caught up in anger, jealousy, resentment, or rage towards others that we forget towards whom the real damage is inflicted upon. In this Chapter, we will see how resentment can affect our internal well-being and how learning to truly forgive others in so many ways leads to a more wholesome and satisfying life.

THE SILENT PROTEST: RESENTMENT

Our egos often misinterpret forgiving others as a sign of giving in to another and because of this we imagine a perceived loss of control. Or perhaps we are afraid to relinquish the upper hand in a relationship or a situation. Just like the philosopher, Friedrich Nietzsche, said,

"It is much more agreeable to offend and later ask forgiveness than to be offended and grant forgiveness."

Some also argue that the act of forgiveness is also easier said than done. What about all those innocent people whose relatives or children have been victimised in acts of hate? Understandably, it is unthinkable for them to forgive those who have caused harm or taken away their loved ones. In fact, it is perfectly plausible to understand how deep bitterness and vindictiveness develops over time in these cases. But unfortunately, it is this type of resentment which becomes a venom that courses through our being, poisoning us long after the emotional wound has healed.

WHAT FORGIVENESS IS NOT

In order to grasp the concept of true forgiveness, we must first warm up our minds to understand what forgiveness is *not*.

First and foremost, the act of forgiving is not forgetting the event or the person that caused you harm. Instead, forgiveness is making a conscious decision to let go of the pain attached to the hurt and suffering, so that you can benefit and your mind can experience vitality and clarity again. When you forgive from within, you clear up emotional hurt so you can experience a resolute sense of peace - and make way for good things to enter your life.

Neither is forgiveness forgoing your boundaries and allowing mistreatment to occur. You must take the appropriate and required action to safeguard your boundaries, at all times. As a trivial example of this, perhaps your friend consistently makes derogatory comments about you in public. You can calmly explain to her later in private, that the way she speaks about you makes you extremely embarrassed and felt let down - and then leave the ball in her court to take the appropriate steps. Here you've taken the action required to protect your boundaries. So in that sense, your slate is clean whether or not he or she takes heed.

I like to think of forgiveness as making a truce with life when you don't get what you want. When we learn to cut the strings of resentment and allow that quiet voice of forgiveness to take over, we suffer less as a result. We can look at people in the eyes, without the emotion of hate. We release the need to be a victim and we do not allow others to feed on our weaknesses. Lastly, we gain control over our lives again. As Buddha wisely once said, "Holding onto anger is like grasping a hot coal with the intent of throwing it at someone else. You are the one who gets burned."

How Pain Begins: The Lure of the Ego

Most adult beings have experienced the ugly wrath of bitterness - especially towards people who have harmed us and caused unnecessary pain in our lives. As infants, we had no inkling of what it meant to be harmed, as our childlike innocence allowed us to trust and love all those around us. But slowly, as we are socialised into a school environment, we learnt that the friend who grabbed our only peach during snack time, also metaphorically took away a small part of our 'identity'. As we watched other loved ones around us suffer, we also learned what it felt like to be hurt. We might have experienced being ostracized because we didn't want to fit into a clique at school. We might have felt hurt to our core as we are called 'piggy' by the popular bully in the playground. Or perhaps we were picked on constantly by a teacher who believed we were not academically apt at the time. We all have these past recollections, which we carry unaware as a subconscious storehouse of memories.

> Think back to your first painful memory at school and observe what that memory does to protect you now. ➤

Initially, these painful memories serve by protecting ourselves from experiencing future pain and disappointment. Eventually however, those 'loyal reminders' might turn into life-long beliefs - and we anchor these painful beliefs into what might be, a very bright future ahead of us.

Say, for example, you are a child in third grade and a popular girl in your class somehow becomes the designated 'group leader'. This meant she could dictate and order to the rest of the girls what they could do or could not do during break and lunch times. Imagine during break-time, this group leader would sit in a chair as a 'make-believe' teacher, and bully all the other girls to sit on the floor around her to listen to her 'pretend lessons' and follow her orders. (True story). Now, although you are only 9 years old, a sudden instinct kicks in and you innately feel uncomfortable with having to conform to someone other than an official authority figure. So you step out of this group. And then for the first time in your life, you experience the pain of what it feels like to be ousted from a group; to feel rejected; and to be teased because you are not 'one of them'. In fact, for the first time in your life, you learn what resentment really feels like. But because your conviction is so strong, you painfully sit alone most of the day with no one to eat with or partner up with. As a result of this, you feel a deep sorrow and develop an understanding that being part of a group is a painful experience, because there always was a chance you could eventually be ostracised. The memory of this experience follows you into your teens and eventually adulthood as you vehemently avoid getting too close to a group of people or being part of a 'clique'. Instead you prefer to branch out, have many friends, and therefore form no real close partnerships.

This kind of experience which led you to have a suspicious belief about group dynamics, halts your potential to eventually develop strong group ties. Until at one point in your adulthood, you realise you possibly could be missing out on the synergy and benefits of being part of a real community.

So for the most part, being wary of group dynamics served you well by preserving your sense of personal power and control - but at what cost? What else could you be missing out on because of this fear? Yes, undoubtedly, learning from the past is essential to how we live our lives in the future - but only as long as the beliefs we develop do not culminate into a strong fear or resentment.

RESENTMENT AND OUR BODY

Louise Hay, a cancer survivor and author of 'You Can Heal Your Life', has long contended that this life-threatening disease is undeniably caused by the effects of a psychological phenomenon - the mind-body relationship.

> Her main premise is that deep resentment held for a long time can literally eat away at the body.

Hay states that people who are later on diagnosed with cancer could have possibly even experienced trauma in their childhood, which destroyed their sense of trust in others and hence led them to find it difficult to develop and maintain long-term, meaningful relationships.[80] These individuals also have a tendency to feel hopeless, helpless and highly self-critical.

More scientific evidence is emerging and one such study is supported by Dr. Luskin as he writes, "When you don't forgive - you release all the chemicals of the stress response. Each time you react, adrenaline, cortisol, and norepinephrine enter the body. When it's a chronic grudge, you could think about it twenty times a day, and those chemicals limit creativity, they limit problem-solving. Cortisol and norepinephrine cause your brain to enter what we call 'the no-thinking zone,' and over time, they lead you to feel helpless and like a victim. When you forgive, you wipe all of that clean."[81]

Psychologist Charlotte Witvliet of *Hope College* performed a study where she asked participants to think about someone who had mistreated or aggrieved them in some way; someone against whom they still held a grudge.[82] Witvliet noted that the 'primary offenders' mostly included romantic partners, friends, and family members. While the participants thought about this person and each of their hurtful actions, Witvliet observed them to note down any physiological reactions specifically, their facial muscle tension, heart rate, blood pressure, and sweat gland activity.

According to Witvliet, thinking about past offenses was a practice of 'un-forgiveness'. She found that when they recalled a grudge, there were very visible and acute physiological changes. Their blood pressure and heart rate increased considerably, and they sweated more. They also reported to Witvliet that they felt less in control.

Gaining Your Power Back

Harbouring resentment is linked to our humanistic tendency of passing judgement on others. Feeling offended, hurt or harmed causes us to push other people away and think of them to be perhaps insensitive, cruel, evil, selfish, arrogant, rude, foolish or more.

> When we judge others, we somewhat gain a sense of self-righteousness and hence feel a sense of false power.

But on a less transient level we also lose out on something very important to our well-being: a sense of inner peace.

For this reason, it is vital to accept that we cannot control the actions of others because all people are essentially victims of their own history, circumstances, and experiences. Everyone's actions are primarily reflected by their own belief systems which have formed inevitably as a result of their past. In fact, perhaps they themselves may be struggling to work on just that very thing they do which irks you. With this understanding, in order to live a life of true contentment - we must learn to detach from other peoples' behaviours and choices, and only focus on what we can control.

Of course, in hindsight, the only thing we can really control are our own attitudes and feelings. By consciously practicing ways not to judge others and to harbour resentments, we can control how we feel in negative situations and choose to remain at peace regardless of the situation. If you think about it:

Wouldn't you rather be internally peaceful as opposed to always being right?

When you let go of this need to judge and be right, not only do you feel lighter and freer but you are also able to develop and maintain more meaningful and deeper relationships with others. As Wayne Dyer poignantly writes in *The 10 Secrets for Success And Inner Peace,* 'a peaceful person attracts peaceful energy'.

BREAKING THE SHACKLES OF RESENTMENT

There is no one magic silver bullet to learning how to really forgive someone. In fact, the practice of forgiveness is so delicate that it can even be described as an art, a science and a power - all combined into one.

According to Dr Wayne Dyer, we practice forgiveness for two reasons,

"One is to let others know that you no longer wish to be in a state of hostility with that person; and two, to free yourself from the self-defeating energy of resentment."[83]

By freeing yourself from the shackles of resentment, you free yourself from negative thoughts and hence you purge the unhealthy emotions residing within your body.

> In this sense, you forgive to lighten your burden as a way to practice self-love.

You also forgive so you can re-connect to other human beings with authenticity and with love — which is the true essence of our being.

There is no cookie-cutter formula, but these few behaviours can help guide you towards learning what it means like to feel true forgiveness:

- **Practice self-care:** First and foremost, true forgiveness cannot be found unless you reconnect with that place inside of you which is whole and complete. You can claim that you have forgiven someone - but until you have really found a place of wholeness and self-love, it will be of a superficial nature and an exercise in futility. Loving and taking care of oneself can be done through many ways like regularly indulging in your passions and hobbies; mixing with people who encourage your spiritual growth; daily exercise; gratitude and prayers; meditation or even volunteer work. Practicing self-nurturing activities is imperative towards maintaining your own peace of mind. This is because once you relax into a more peaceful state of mind, only then can you express authentic joy and love towards others. It's like that old adage which we have read time and time again, "You can't pour from an empty cup. Take care of yourself first." The bottom line is - the better care you take of yourselves, the easier it is to release resentments.

- **Stand in their Shoes (for Even A Minute):** Scientific research points to the fact that empathy and forgiveness go hand-in-hand. Quite naturally when someone hurts us or crosses our personal boundaries - disdain or anger immediately takes over, and our barriers jump back into place. In the heat of the moment, we forget that the person's past experience could have lead them to this space of hurt. But going to a quiet space, closing your eyes and making a conscious effort to understand where they are coming from, can actually miraculously ease the burning desire to judge. Begin by asking yourself,

When you have the intention of really understanding the other person, you become free from the prison of your own views. In one study, a group of people were asked to judge the fairness of a misconduct and then consider whether to forgive it or empathise with the transgressor. The participants evaluated several such social scenarios while the researchers scanned their brain activity through MRI machines. Researchers found that the areas which were located deep in the emotional centres of the brain lit up when participants empathised with or forgave transgressors. This was in contrast to activity in the region of the brain associated with 'reasoning', when judging the fairness of a situation. What this study means is that, in order to learn how to forgive, we must avoid judging the fairness of the situation and instead, try to empathise by seeing things from the perspective of those who hurt us.

- **Pray for Them:** The next step (and perhaps the most powerful) in forgiving someone else is to pray for the person who wronged you. Jesus said, "Love your enemies and pray for those who persecute you" (Matthew 5:44). Having experienced this beautiful and magical process myself many a time, I can unquestionably endorse it. Recently, an acquaintance attempted to thwart a potential business plan of mine and naturally, I was seething with resentment. As I sat on the dining table with my husband, I ranted on how I knew from the start not to trust this lady. As I could feel myself getting more enraged, I knew right then and there what I needed to do. I needed to find a quiet space, sit down and then pray for guidance to let go of this anger festering within. And then I proceeded to do what was most counterintuitive. As I sat quietly, I actually prayed for my acquaintance's well-being. And this is where the real switch happened. It was only then that I began to see that this lady was struggling, and doing her best to maintain her career. I could see her in the present day looking for ways to support her family and also feeling lost. Feeling a little bit of sympathy, I began to pray for an improvement in her well-being and happiness. Not only did I come out feeling so much lighter and peaceful, I also found that at least eighty percent of my resentment literally disappeared. I was not to forget her actions, and would still be wary of her.

> But, at least my serenity was saved.

It was really that simple. Praying for others not only breaks the chain of resentment and bitterness, but it miraculously leaves you feeling whole and at peace.

If however, you are really struggling to make peace with someone, you can also practice repeatedly reciting this simple Buddhist prayer in your heart:

If I have harmed any one in any way, either knowingly or unknowingly through my own confusions, I ask their forgiveness. If anyone has harmed me in any way, either knowingly or unknowingly through their own confusions, I forgive them. And if there is a situation, I am not yet ready to forgive, I forgive myself for that. For all the ways that I harm myself, negate, doubt, belittle myself, judge or be unkind to myself, through my own confusions, I forgive myself.[84]

SUMMARY

Not being able to forgive others has disturbing consequences for our well-being and robs us of our inner peace. Not only does it limit our development or growth because we are kept in a place of hate, but more and more evidence points out that holding onto resentment can also pose serious health risks.

The area where we get most stuck while releasing resentment is in our perception of others - also known as 'judgement'. If we keep in mind that we cannot control people's behaviour, we can learn to let go of the need to judge.

Here is a three-pronged approach to forgive someone who has hurt you:

- **Real self-care:** Once you relax into a more peaceful state of mind through taking care of yourself, only then can you genuinely have the space to forgive from a place of well-being.
- **Using Your Empathy Muscle:** Being able to stand in their shoes and understand where they come from, can ease the burning desire to judge and carry resentment. Begin by asking, **"What past experience is making them respond in this way?"**
- **Pray for Them:** This is where a powerful shift in forgiveness resides. When you wish well for the person who has hurt you and it comes from a genuine place - forgiveness becomes much easier and more real.

REFERENCES

[1] C. L. M. Keyes, D. Shmotkin and C. D. Ryff, "Optimizing well-being: The empirical encounter of two traditions," *Journal of Personality and Social Psychology* 82, no. 6 (2002) 1007-1022, doi: 10.1037/0022-3514.82.6.1007.

[2] Ryan, R.M., & Deci, E.L, "On happiness and human potentials: a review of research on hedonic and eudaimonic well-being," *Annual Review of Psychology* 52, (2001): 141-66, doi: 10.1146/annurev.psych.52.1.141.

[3] A. S. Waterman, "Two conceptions of happiness: Contrasts of personal expressiveness (eudaimonia) and hedonic enjoyment," *Journal of Personality and Social Psychology* 64, no. 4 (1993): 678-691, doi:10.1037/0022-3514.64.4.678.

[4] David Myers, *The Pursuit of Happiness* (New York: Morrow, 1992).

[5]

[6] Baumeister, Roy F. *Self-regulation and Self-control: Selected Works of Roy F. Baumeister*. Abingdon, Oxon: Routledge, 2018.

[7] Jasongots. *"The Neuroscience of Success."* Big Think. August 04, 2011. https://bigthink.com/think-tank/the-neuroscience-of-success.

[8] Steel, Piers. *The Nature of Procrastination: A Meta-Analytic and Theoretical Review of Quintessential Self-Regulatory Failure.* University of Calgary, 2007. Psychological Bulletin, The American Psychological Association, 2007. Vol. 133. No.1, 65-94.

[9] Whitbourne, Susan Krauss, Ph.D. *"A New Way to Understand Procrastination."* Psychology Today. January 09, 2018. https://www.psychologytoday.com/us/blog/fulfillment-any-age/201801/new-way-understand-procrastination.

[10] Ware, Deann, Ph.D. "Neurons That Fire Together Wire Together." Psychologist's Guide to Emotional Well Being. https://www.dailyshoring.com/neurons-that-fire-together-wire-together/.

[11] Newport, Cal. Deep Work. London: Piatkus, 2016.

[12] Newport, Cal. Deep Work. London: Piatkus, 2016.

[13] Brigid Schulte, *Overwhelmed: Work, Love, and Play When No One Has the Time* (London: Picador, 2015), 268

[14] Quoted in Emma Seppälä, *The Happiness Track: How to Apply the Science of Happiness to Accelerate Your Success* (New York: Harper Collins, 2017).

[15] Osho, *Creativity: Unleashing the Forces Within* (New York: St. Martin's Press, 1999), 146.

[16]"Mental health in the workplace," World Health Organization, September 2017, http://www.who.int/mental_health/in_the_workplace/en/.
[17]Ibid

[18] https://onlinelibrary.wiley.com/doi/abs/10.1111/j.1467-8691.1992.tb00052.x

[19] "Facts & Statistics," Anxiety and Depression Association of America, accessed on October 13, 2018, https://adaa.org/about-adaa/press-room/facts-statistics.

[20]http://edition.cnn.com/2011/HEALTH/07/28/ep.smartphone.obsessed.cohen/index.htm

[21] John H. Morrison et al, "Stress-Induced Dendritic Remodeling in the Prefrontal Cortex is Circuit Specific," *Cerebral Cortex* 19, no.10 (2009): 2479–2484, doi: 10.1093/cercor/bhp003.

[22] Mihaly Csikszentmihalyi, *Flow: The Psychology of Optimal Experience* (New York: HarperCollins, 2008), 3.

[23] Steven Kotler, "Flow States and Creativity," *Psychology Today*, February 25, 2014, https://www.psychologytoday.com/us/blog/the-playing-field/201402/flow-states-and-creativity.

[24] Nicholas A. Turiano, Avron Spiro III, and Daniel Mroczek, "Openness to Experience and Mortality in Men: Analysis of Trait and Facets," *Journal of Aging and Health* 24, no. 4 (2012): 654-672, doi: 10.1177/0898264311431303

[25] David Burkus, *The Myths of Creativity: The Truth About How Innovative Companies and People Generate Great Ideas* (San Fracisco: Wiley, 2014), 25.

[26] Emma Seppälä, *The Happiness Track: How to Apply the Science of Happiness to Accelerate Your Success* (New York: Harper Collins, 2017)

[27] Joos Meyer, "Alpha Brain Waves – The science behind peak performance and creativity," DawnGrant, September 9, 2017, https://dawngrant.com/blogs/dawn-grant-blog/alpha-brain-waves-the-science-behind-peak-performance-and-creativity.

[28] Mareike Wieth and Rose Zacks, "Time of day effects on problem solving: When the non-optimal is optimal," *Thinking and Reasoning* 17, no. 4 (2011): 387-401, doi: 10.1080/13546783.2011.625663.

[29] Cindi May, "The Inspiration Paradox: Your Best Creative Time Is Not When You Think," Scientific American Online, March 6, 2012.

[30] Jan Brogan, "When being distracted is a good thing," Boston Online, February 27, 2012, http://archive.boston.com/lifestyle/health/articles/2012/02/27/when_being_distracted_is_a_good_thing/.

[31] Ruth Ann Atchley, David L. Strayer, and Paul Atchley, "Creativity in the Wild: Improving Creative Reasoning through Immersion in Natural Settings," PLoS ONE 7, no. 12 (2012): e51474, doi: 10.1371/journal. pone.0051474

[32] Emma Seppälä, *The Happiness Track: How to Apply the Science of Happiness to Accelerate Your Success* (New York: Harper Collins, 2017)

[33] Festinger, Leon. A Theory of Cognitive Dissonance. Stanford, CA: Stanford University Press, 2009.

[34] Borchard, Therese. "Top 5 Hidden Causes of Depression." Thereseborchard.com. April 20, 2015. http://thereseborchard. com/2015/04/20/treating-the-underlying-causes-of-depression-an-interview-with-integrative-doctor-alan-weiss/.

[35] Ferrucci, Piero, and Vivien Ferrucci. The Power of Kindness: The Unexpected Benefits of Leading a Compassionate Life. NY, NY: TarcherPerigee, an Imprint of Penguin Random House LLC, 2016.

[36] McKay, Brett, and Kate McKay. "What Strengthens and Weakens Our Integrity - Part I: Why Small Choices Count." The Art of Manliness. August 5, 2018. https://www.artofmanliness.com/articles/what-strengthens-and-weakens-our-integrity-part-i-why-small-choices-count/.

[37] Damasio, Antoino R. "Emotion, Decision Making and the Orbitofrontal Cortex." In Cerebral Cortex, 295-307. 3rd ed. Vol. 10. 2000.

[38] Marshall, Charles W. Shattering the Glass Slipper: Destroying Fairy-tale Thinking before It Destroys You. Prominent Pub., 2002.

[39] Ruiz, Miguel, and Janet Mills. The Four Agreements. Thorndike, Me.: Center Point Pub., 2008.

[40] Weller, Chris. "A Neuroscientist Who Studies Decision-making Reveals the Most Important Choice You Can Make." Business Insider. July 28, 2017. https://www.businessinsider.in/A-neuroscientist-who-studies-decision-making-reveals-the-most-important-choice-you-can-make/articleshow/59812746.cms.

[41] Bonesio, John. "Is Our Side of the Street Clean?" Simply Great Lives. February 25, 2015. https://simplygreatlives.com/our-calling/is-our-side-of-the-street-clean/.

[42] Newman, Susan. The Book of No: 200 Ways to Say It - and Mean It and Stop People-pleasing Forever. New York: McGraw-Hill, 2005.

[43] Alfred, Lord Tennyson, *Idylls of the King* (New York: Penguin Classics, 1989).

[44]

[45] Piero Ferrucci and Vivien Ferrucci, *The Power of Kindness: The Unexpected Benefits of Leading a Compassionate Life* (New York: Penguin Random House, 2016).

[46] "Jonathan Sacks, "Beha'alotcha (5768) – Humility," Rabbi Sacks, April 04, 2016, http://rabbisacks.org/covenant-conversation-5768-behaalotcha-humility/.

[47] G. T. Doran, "There's a S.M.A.R.T. way to write management's goals and objectives," *Management Review*, AMA FORUM 70, no. 11(1981): 35–36.

[48] Russ Harris, *The Happiness Trap* (Boston: Trumpeter, 2008), 167.

[49] Ibid.

[50] https://medium.com/littlephilnews/helping-others-releases-the-same-hormones-as-sex-d2fb8c51cf41

[51] Pat Donovan, "Study finds it actually is better (and healthier) to give than to receive," University of Buffalo, February 4, 2013, http://www.buffalo.edu/news/releases/2013/02/003.html.

[52] Hanson, Rick. "Take in the Good." Dr. Rick Hanson. July 29, 2018. Accessed September 27, 2018. https://www.rickhanson.net/take-in-the-good/.

[53] Osho. Body Mind Balancing. Griffin Publishing, 2005.

[54] Kirsti A. Dyer, "Butterflies & Blazes," Journey of Hearts, December 1, 1998, https://journeyofhearts.org/kirstimd/bflycocoon.htm

[55] Steve Taylor, "Transformation Through Suffering: A Study of Individuals Who Have Experienced Positive Psychological Transformation Following Periods of Intense Turmoil," *Journal of Humanistic Psychology* 52, no. 1 (2012): 30-52, doi: 10.1177/0022167811404944

[56] Ibid.

[57] Jon Kabat-Zinn, *Coming to Our Senses: Healing Ourselves and the World Through Mindfulness* (NY: Hachette Books, 2006), 407.

[58] Marcus Aurelius, *Meditations* (New York: Penguin, 2006).

[59] Gary Klein, *Seeing What Others Don't: The Remarkable Ways We Gain Insights* (London: Nicholas Brealey Publishing, 2017).

[60] Thomas Oppong, "The Formula For Success That's Been Followed by The Icons of History," *Medium*, May 10, 2017, https://medium.com/personal-growth/the-formula-for-success-thats-been-followed-by-the-icons-of-history-dfdc0a8e6d10.

[61] Donald Pfaff, *The Altruistic Brain: How We Are Naturally Good* (New York: Oxford University Press, 2015), 3.

[62] Ibid., 10.

[63] Sören Krach et al., "Your Flaws Are My Pain: Linking Empathy To Vicarious Embarrassment," PLoS ONE 6, no. 4 (2011): e18675, doi: 10.1371/journal.pone.0018675.

[64] Sandra Blakeslee, "Cells That Read Minds," The New York Times Online, January 10, 2006, https://www.nytimes.com/2006/01/10/science/cells-that-read-minds.html.

[65] Robert Hepach, Amrisha Vaish, and Michael Tomasello, "Young Children Are Intrinsically Motivated to See Others Helped," *Psychology Science* 23, no. 9 (2012): 967-72, doi: 10.1177/0956797612440571.

[66] Elizabeth W. Dunn, Lara B. Aknin, and Michael I. Norton, "Spending Money on Others Promotes Happiness," *Science* 319, no. 5870 (2008): 1687-1688, doi: 10.1126/science.1150952.

[67] Allan Luks and Peggy Payne, *The Healing Power of Doing Good: The Health and Spiritual Benefits of Helping Others* (Lincoln: iUniverse.com, Inc., 2001), 49.

[68] Elizabeth Renter, "What Generosity Does to Your Brain and Life Expectancy," U.S. News, May 1, 2015, https://health.usnews.com/health-news/health-wellness/articles/2015/05/01/what-generosity-does-to-your-brain-and-life-expectancy.

[69] Piero Ferrucci, *The Power of Kindness: The Unexpected Benefits of Leading a Compassionate Life* (New York: Penguin Random House, 2016).

[70] Felix Warnekin and Michael Tomasello, "Extrinsic rewards undermine altruistic tendencies in 20-month-olds," *Developmental Psychology* 44, no. 6 (2008): 1785-1788, doi: 10.1037/a0013860.

[71] James H. Fowler, and Nicholas A. Christakis, "Cooperative behavior cascades in human social networks," *Proceedings of the National Academy of Sciences of the United States of America* 107, no. 12 (2010): 5334-5338, doi: 10.1073/pnas.0913149107.

[72] Abraham Maslow, *The Farther Reaches of Human Nature* (New York: Penguin Random House, 1993), 34-35.

[73] Jacob Olesen, "Fear of Success Phobia – Achievemephobia," FearOf.Net, https://www.fearof.net/fear-of-success-phobia-achievemephobia/.

[74] Abraham Maslow, *Motivation and Personality* (New Delhi: Pearson Education, 1987), 64.

[75] Abraham Maslow, "A theory of Human Motivation," *Psychological Review* 50, no. 4 (1943): 370-396, doi: 10.1037/h0054346.

[76] Susanne Babbel, "Fear of Success," Psychology Today, January 03, 2011, https://www.psychologytoday.com/us/blog/somatic-psychology/201101/fear-success.

[77] Clance, Pauline Rose, and Suzanne Ament Imes. "The Imposter Phenomenon in High Achieving Women: Dynamics and Therapeutic Intervention." Psychotherapy: Theory, Research & Practice 15, no. 3 (1978): 241-47.

[78] Cho, William. "The Jonah Complex - Fear of Your Own Greatness – Student Voices." Student Voices. December 06, 2017. https://mystudentvoices.com/the-jonah-complex-fear-of-your-own-greatness-47d9e8d41ab5.

[79] http://www.parentsofprodigals.com/letting-go/

[80] Louise Hay, *You Can Heal Your Life* (California: Hay House, 2004).
[81] Megan Feldman Bettencourt, *Triumph of the Heart: Forgiveness in an Unforgiving World* (New York: Penguin Random House LLC, 2015), 37.
[82] Charlotte Van Oyen Witvliet et al. "Granting Forgiveness or Harboring Grudges: Implications for Emotion, Physiology, and Health," *Psychological Science* 12, no. 2 (2001): 117-123, doi: 10.1111/1467-9280.00320.
[83] Wayne W. Dyer, *21 Days to Master Success and Inner Peace* (UK: Hay House, 2011), Kindle.
[84] Rinki Srivatsav, "A Buddhist prayer of forgiveness," *The Speaking Tree*, July 31, 2013. https://www.speakingtree.in/allslides/a-buddhist-prayer-of-forgiveness

Bibliography

Dyer, Wayne W. *21 Days to Master Success and Inner Peace*. UK: Hay House, 2011. Kindle.

Iacoboni, Marco. "Imitation, Empathy and Mirror Neurons." *Annual Review of Psychology* 60, (2009): 653-670. doi: 10.1146/annurev.psych.60.110707.163604.

Kounios, John. "The Neuroscience Behind Epiphanies." *TED Talks Talent Search*. Video. https://www.youtube.com/watch?v=7uyw5y_tHEM.

Kounios, John, and Mark Beeman. "The Aha! Moment: the Neural Basis of Solving Problems with Insight." *PLOS Biology* 18, no. 4 (2009): e111. doi: 10.1371/journal.pbio.0020111.

Miller, R.S. "Empathic embarrassment: Situational and personal determinants of reactions to the embarrassment of another." *Journal of Personality and Social Psychology* 53, (1987): 1061–1069. doi: 10.1037/0022-3514.53.6.1061.

Marcus, D.K., Wilson, J.R., Miller, R.S. "Are Perceptions of Emotion in the Eye of the Beholder? A Social Relations Analysis of Judgments of Embarrassment." *Personality Social Psychology Bulletin* 22, (1996): 1220–1228. doi: 10.1177/01461672962212003.

Phillips, Nicky. "Taking a Break is Secret to Success." *Sydney Morning Herald*. August 16, 2012. https://www.smh.com.au/education/taking-a-break-is-secret-to-success-20120815-24951.html.

Shearn, D., Spellman, L., Meirick, J., and Stryker, K. "Empathic blushing in friends and strangers." *Motivation & Emotion* 23, (1999): 307–316. doi: 10.1023/A:1021342910378.

Worthington Jr., Everett L. "The New Science of Forgiveness." *Greater Good Magazine*. September 1, 2004.

Burton, Neel, M.D. "What's the Difference Between Modesty and Humility?" Psychology Today. https://www.psychologytoday.com/au/blog/hide-and-seek/201806/whats-the-difference-between-modesty-and-humility.

Hanson, Rick. "Confronting the Negativity Bias." Dr. Rick Hanson. May 26, 2017. https://www.rickhanson.net/how-your-brain-makes-you-easily-intimidated/.

«How Meditation Strengthens Your Willpower, Self-Control, Discipline.» EOC Institute. https://eocinstitute.org/meditation/boosting-willpower-self-discipline/.

Parvez, Hanan. "PsychMechanics." What Makes a Person Stubborn. https://www.psychmechanics.com/2014/08/beliefs-programs-of-subconscious-mind.html.

Acknowledgements

This book would have never happened without the encouragement of my 11 year old well-heeled and savvy Samara, who insisted I write a book on the topic Happiness. If it weren't for you - this book would have never happened.

I also owe Yaash, my young son, for our endless deep and insightful conversations about life, existentialism and pain- which inspired so much of my writing. Your intuition is beyond measure.

Vishal, for being the most and steady consistent pillar - silently always charading me from behind the scenes.

Printed in Great Britain
by Amazon